AF413545

Start Smart India

Launch Your Business with Confidence

Content:

~~~~~~~

Gururbrahma Gururvishnuh,

Gururdevo Maheshwarah |

Guruhsakshat Parabrahma,

Tasmai Shrigurave Namah ||

~~~~~~~

In the vast tapestry of Hindu mythology, Lord Vishnu stands as a pillar of stability and righteousness, revered for his role as the preserver and sustainer of the universe. His divine presence symbolizes harmony, order, and prosperity, making him a beacon of hope and inspiration for humanity.

In the context of business establishment and life, the significance of Lord Vishnu transcends mere religious beliefs; it encompasses timeless wisdom and principles that are profoundly relevant to our modern-day endeavors. As the preserver of dharma (righteousness) and karma (action), Lord Vishnu exemplifies the essence of ethical conduct, integrity, and balance.

In the journey of entrepreneurship delineated within this book, invoking the grace of Lord Vishnu is akin to seeking divine guidance and blessings for success and fulfillment. Just as Vishnu meticulously upholds the cosmic order, entrepreneurs are called upon to uphold ethical standards, honor commitments, and foster harmony within their ventures and communities.

Furthermore, Lord Vishnu's iconic form of Lord Narayana, reclining on the cosmic serpent Adi Shesha, represents the state of deep restful awareness and consciousness. This symbolizes the importance of introspection, strategic planning, and aligning actions with a higher purpose in both business and life.

Moreover, Lord Vishnu is often depicted holding the Sudarshana Chakra, a powerful weapon symbolizing the pursuit of truth and justice. In the realm of business, this conveys the importance of integrity, fairness, and adherence to moral principles, even in the face of adversity.

As entrepreneurs embark on their journey, may they draw inspiration from the divine qualities of Lord Vishnu, cultivating humility, perseverance, and a sense of duty towards their endeavors. By aligning their actions with the timeless wisdom embodied by Vishnu, entrepreneurs can navigate challenges with grace, foster sustainable growth, and contribute positively to the world around them.

May the blessings of Lord Vishnu illuminate the path of entrepreneurship outlined within this book, guiding aspiring business owners towards prosperity, fulfillment, and enduring success.

~ Jai Shri Vishnu Ji

~~~~~~~~~~~~~
~~~~~~~~~~~~~

THANK YOU!

To my family,

This book is dedicated to you- my pillars of strength, unwavering support, and endless inspiration. Through every twist and turn of this entrepreneurial journey, you have been my rock, standing by me with boundless love, encouragement, and understanding.

Your belief in my dreams, your sacrifices, and your unwavering faith have been the driving force behind every milestone achieved and every challenge overcome. You have cheered me on during moments of triumph and lifted me up during moments of doubt. Your presence in my life is a constant reminder of what truly matters - family, love, and shared dreams.

As I embark on this venture into the world of entrepreneurship, I carry with me the values, lessons, and memories that we have shared together. Your unwavering support fuels my passion, your wisdom guides my decisions, and your love empowers me to strive for greatness.

This book is not just a culmination of my efforts; it is a testament to the love, dedication, and sacrifices of each and every one of you. May its pages serve as a reminder of the journey we have shared and the dreams we continue to pursue together.

& To my dear wife Kaamna Parashar (CS, LL.M.)

Thank you for always being a great guide, standing by me, especially during the toughest of days. Your unwavering support and love have been my rock, and I am grateful for you every single day.

With deepest gratitude and love, Gagan

ABOUT AUTHOR

Gagan Parashar (GP) is a seasoned Brand and Business Consultant with a remarkable track record spanning over 15 years in the industry. Based in NCR, India, Gagan's expertise covers a wide spectrum of areas, including the successful ownership and operation of a bootstrap business and brand consulting firm.

Throughout his illustrious career, Gagan has had the privilege of collaborating with esteemed clients from across the globe. His client roster includes renowned names such as Softbank in Japan, Financial Artisan (Japan), Philips India, Havells India, and Hager India, among others. Gagan's clientele extends beyond borders, with notable engagements with companies like Gulf Ferro Alloys Company (SABAYEK) in Dubai, AJM Kooheji Group (Dubai), and Dar Wa Emaar (Dubai).

Gagan's diverse portfolio showcases his versatility and proficiency in undertaking a multitude of research assignments across various industries and companies. His responsibilities have ranged from analyzing complex business requirements to providing strategic advisory solutions through detailed research reports. Gagan's expertise encompasses company profiling, competitor analysis, strategy development, industry assessment, market landscaping, stakeholder analysis, and regulatory requirements analysis.

In addition to his research prowess, Gagan has been deeply involved in overseeing strategic business initiatives, executing operational and marketing plans, and developing and implementing standard operating procedures (SOPs).

His role has also extended to quality assurance and management communication, where he has been instrumental in conducting quality checks, preparing management communications, generating service level reports, and spearheading business development initiatives.

With his wealth of experience, honed skills, and extensive knowledge, Gagan Parashar is a trusted partner for businesses seeking to enhance their brand presence, optimize operational efficiency, and drive sustainable growth. His commitment to excellence and proven track record makes him a valuable asset in achieving organizational success.

~~~~~~~~~~
~~~~~~~~~~

FOREWORD

In today's dynamic and ever-evolving business landscape, aspiring entrepreneurs are faced with a multitude of challenges and opportunities as they embark on their journey of establishing their businesses. From navigating market complexities to ensuring legal compliance and fostering sustainable growth, the path to entrepreneurial success can be both exhilarating and daunting.

This forward-thinking guide offers a comprehensive roadmap for novice entrepreneurs seeking to navigate the Indian business terrain with confidence and clarity. Drawing from a wealth of industry experience and insights garnered from esteemed organizations across the globe, this book provides invaluable guidance on every aspect of starting and scaling a business in India.

From the initial stages of ideation and market research to the complexities of financial planning, branding and marketing strategy, and operations management, this guide equips aspiring entrepreneurs with the knowledge, tools, and strategies needed to thrive in today's competitive landscape. Through practical examples, case studies, and actionable advice, readers are inspired to think creatively, adapt proactively, and embrace change as they embark on their entrepreneurial journey.

Whether you're a budding entrepreneur with a game-changing idea or an aspiring business owner seeking to expand your horizons, this guide will serve as your trusted companion, guiding you towards entrepreneurial excellence and sustainable growth.

Here's to your success,

~~~~~~~~~~~~~~~~
~~~~~~~~~~~~~~~~

PREFACE

Welcome to the world of entrepreneurship, where dreams are forged into reality, and innovation knows no bounds.

In this ever-evolving landscape of business, embarking on the journey of entrepreneurship can be both exhilarating and daunting. From the initial spark of an idea to the day-to-day challenges of running a successful enterprise, the path is filled with twists, turns, and unexpected opportunities.

This book, "Comprehensive Guide to Starting a Business in India," is a culmination of years of experience, research, and insights tailored specifically for beginners venturing into the world of business in India. Whether you're a budding entrepreneur with a game-changing concept or an aspiring business owner seeking guidance on navigating the intricacies of the Indian market, this guide is designed to be your trusted companion.

Starting with an exploration of the entrepreneurial mindset and the fundamentals of business planning, we delve into the legal, financial, and operational aspects of setting up and running a business in India. From understanding market dynamics to crafting effective branding and marketing strategies, each chapter offers practical advice, actionable steps, and real-world examples to empower you on your entrepreneurial journey.

As you journey through the pages of this book, you'll discover insights on location selection, infrastructure setup, human resources management, technology adoption, and risk management strategies tailored to the Indian business landscape. Moreover, you'll find guidance on scaling and expanding your business, building a sustainable enterprise, and navigating legal and compliance requirements in India.

This book is not just a manual; it's a roadmap—a roadmap to help you navigate the twists and turns of entrepreneurship.

with confidence, resilience, and a relentless pursuit of excellence. Whether you're dreaming of launching the next big startup or seeking to build a thriving small business, let this guide be your compass as you embark on this transformative journey.

Remember, entrepreneurship is not just about building businesses; it's about creating impact, fostering innovation, and leaving a lasting legacy. So, seize the opportunity, embrace the challenges, and embark on this exhilarating adventure with courage and determination.

Here's to your success!

~~~~~~~~~~~~~~~~
~~~~~~~~~~~~~~~~

ACKNOWLEDGMENT

We extend our heartfelt gratitude to everyone who contributed to the creation of this book, "Start Smart India: Launching Your Business with Confidence."

First and foremost, we would like to thank the countless entrepreneurs, business leaders, and industry experts whose invaluable insights and experiences have enriched the content of this guide. Your wisdom, expertise, and willingness to share your knowledge have been instrumental in shaping the narrative and providing readers with practical advice and actionable strategies. We are deeply appreciative of our clients and collaborators who have entrusted us with their business challenges and opportunities over the years. Your partnership, trust, and support have been the driving force behind our continued growth and success.

A special thanks to the team at Publishing House for their dedication, professionalism, and commitment to excellence throughout the publishing process. Your expertise in editing, design, and production has helped bring this book to life and ensure its quality and impact.

We would also like to express our gratitude to our families and loved ones for their unwavering support, encouragement, and understanding during the writing process. Your patience, love, and belief in our vision have been our greatest source of strength and inspiration.

Last but not least, we extend our heartfelt thanks to the readers of this book. It is our sincere hope that the knowledge and insights shared within these pages will empower you on your entrepreneurial journey and inspire you to launch and grow your business with confidence. *With gratitude, GP!*

Part I: Getting Started
~~~~~~~~~~~~~~~~
~~~~~~~~~~~~~~~~

1.1　Understanding the Entrepreneurial Mindset

Embarking on the journey of entrepreneurship requires more than just a great idea—it demands a unique mindset characterized by innovation, resilience, and adaptability. In this chapter, we delve into the core principles of the entrepreneurial mindset, exploring what sets successful entrepreneurs apart and how you can cultivate these traits within yourself.

What is the Entrepreneurial Mindset?

The entrepreneurial mindset is a mindset characterized by a unique set of attitudes, beliefs, and behaviors that enable individuals to identify opportunities, take calculated risks, and navigate uncertainty with confidence. It involves a combination of creativity, resourcefulness, and a willingness to embrace challenges as opportunities for growth.

Key Traits of the Entrepreneurial Mindset:

1. **Creativity and Innovation:** Successful entrepreneurs possess a knack for thinking outside the box and finding innovative solutions to problems. They are constantly seeking new ideas and approaches to disrupt the status quo.

2. **Resilience and Perseverance:** Entrepreneurship is a journey filled with ups and downs. Those with an entrepreneurial mindset are resilient in the face of setbacks, viewing failures as learning opportunities and bouncing back stronger than ever.

3. **Adaptability and Flexibility:** The ability to adapt to changing circumstances and pivot when necessary is

crucial for entrepreneurial success. Entrepreneurs with an entrepreneurial mindset are agile and flexible, adjusting their strategies as needed to stay ahead of the curve.

4. **Risk-Taking and Courage:** Entrepreneurship inherently involves risk, and those with an entrepreneurial mindset are not afraid to take calculated risks in pursuit of their goals. They possess the courage to step outside their comfort zones and embrace uncertainty.

5. **Vision and Goal-Orientation:** Entrepreneurs with an entrepreneurial mindset have a clear vision for the future and set ambitious goals to achieve it. They are driven by a sense of purpose and are committed to realizing their dreams.

Cultivating the Entrepreneurial Mindset:

- **Practice Creative Thinking:** Engage in activities that stimulate creativity, such as brainstorming sessions, mind mapping, or exposure to diverse perspectives.

- **Embrace Failure:** Reframe failures as opportunities for growth and learning. Adopt a growth mindset that views setbacks as stepping-stones to success.

- **Seek Feedback:** Solicit feedback from mentors, peers, and customers to gain insights and refine your ideas and strategies.

- **Stay Curious:** Cultivate a lifelong learning mindset by staying curious and seeking **new** knowledge and experiences.

- **Take Action:** Don't wait for the perfect moment—take action and iterate as you go. Embrace experimentation and be willing to pivot when necessary.

Understanding the entrepreneurial mindset is the foundation for success in entrepreneurship. By embracing creativity, resilience, adaptability, and a willingness to take risks, aspiring entrepreneurs can cultivate the mindset needed to thrive in today's dynamic business landscape. With dedication, perseverance, and a relentless pursuit of innovation, you can unlock your full potential and achieve entrepreneurial greatness.

~~~~~~~~~~~~~~~
~~~~~~~~~~~~~~~

Chapter 1: Introduction to Entrepreneurship

1.2 Exploring the Motivation to Start a Business

Before embarking on the entrepreneurial journey, it's essential to explore the motivations driving your desire to start a business. Understanding your underlying reasons for entrepreneurship will not only guide your decision-making process but also fuel your passion and determination along the way. In this chapter, we delve into the various motivations that inspire individuals to become entrepreneurs and how to harness these motivations to achieve success.

Identifying Your Motivations:

1. **Passion and Purpose:** Many entrepreneurs are driven by a deep-seated passion for a particular industry, product, or cause. They are motivated by the desire to make a meaningful impact and pursue their interests on their own terms.

2. **Financial Independence:** For some individuals, entrepreneurship represents an opportunity to achieve financial independence and build wealth. They are motivated by the prospect of controlling their financial destiny and creating opportunities for themselves and their families.

3. **Autonomy and Freedom:** Entrepreneurship offers a level of autonomy and freedom that traditional employment often cannot provide. Entrepreneurs are motivated by the desire to be their own boss, set their own schedule, and pursue their vision without constraints.

4. **Desire for Innovation:** Many entrepreneurs are driven by a desire to innovate and disrupt the status quo. They are motivated by the opportunity to create something new, solve pressing problems, and leave a lasting impact on their industry or community.

5. **Personal Growth and Fulfillment:** Entrepreneurship is a journey of personal growth and self-discovery. Some individuals are motivated by the challenge of pushing themselves out of their comfort zones, overcoming obstacles, and achieving their full potential.

Harnessing Your Motivations:

- **Reflect on Your Values:** Take time to reflect on your core values, interests, and long-term goals. Identify how entrepreneurship aligns with your values and what you hope to achieve through your business venture.

- **Set Clear Goals:** Establish clear and specific goals for your business, both short-term and long-term. Having a clear vision of what you want to accomplish will keep you motivated and focused on your journey.

- **Seek Inspiration:** Surround yourself with sources of inspiration and motivation, whether it's through books, podcasts, mentors, or networking events. Connect with other entrepreneurs who share similar motivations and learn from their experiences.

- **Stay Flexible:** Recognize that motivations may evolve over time as you progress on your entrepreneurial journey. Stay open to new opportunities and be willing to adapt your goals and strategies accordingly.

Exploring your motivations to start a business is the first step towards building a successful venture. By understanding what drives you and harnessing that motivation to fuel your entrepreneurial journey, you can overcome challenges, stay focused on your goals, and ultimately achieve success on your own terms. Whether your motivation is driven by passion, financial independence, autonomy, innovation, or personal growth, embrace it wholeheartedly and let it guide you towards entrepreneurial greatness.

~~~~~~~~~~~~~~~~~~~~~~~~~~~
~~~~~~~~~~~~~~~~~~~~~~~~~~~

1.3 Debunking Common Myths and Misconceptions about Entrepreneurship

Before diving headfirst into the world of entrepreneurship, it's crucial to separate fact from fiction and debunk common myths and misconceptions that may hinder your journey. In this chapter, we dispel some of the most prevalent myths surrounding entrepreneurship and provide clarity on what it truly takes to succeed as an entrepreneur.

Myth #1: Entrepreneurship is Only for Risk-Takers

- **Reality:** While entrepreneurship does involve taking risks, successful entrepreneurs are not reckless gamblers. They are strategic risk-takers who carefully assess opportunities and mitigate potential downsides through thorough planning and analysis.

Myth #2: Entrepreneurs Must Have a Revolutionary Idea

- **Reality:** Not every successful business is built on a groundbreaking idea. Many successful entrepreneurs find success by identifying niche markets, improving existing products or services, or addressing common pain points in innovative ways.

Myth #3: Entrepreneurship Guarantees Instant Success

- **Reality:** Entrepreneurship is a journey filled with highs and lows, and success rarely happens overnight. It takes time, dedication, and perseverance to build a successful business.

Overnight successes are often the result of years of hard work and persistence behind the scenes.

Myth #4: You Need a Large Amount of Capital to Start a Business

- **Reality:** While having access to capital can certainly accelerate the growth of your business, many successful entrepreneurs have started with minimal funds. Bootstrapping, seeking alternative financing options, and focusing on lean startup principles can help you launch and grow your business without breaking the bank.

Myth #5: Entrepreneurs Work Less and Have More Free Time

- **Reality:** While entrepreneurship offers flexibility and autonomy, it also requires hard work, dedication, and long hours, especially in the early stages. Successful entrepreneurs are often the first ones in and the last ones out, putting in the necessary effort to build and grow their businesses.

Dispelling the Myths:

- **Seek Mentorship:** Connect with experienced entrepreneurs who can provide guidance and insights based on their own experiences.

- **Educate Yourself:** Stay informed about the realities of entrepreneurship through books, podcasts, courses, and networking events.

- **Focus on Execution:** Instead of waiting for the perfect moment or idea, take action and iterate as you go. Execution is key to success in entrepreneurship.

By debunking common myths and misconceptions about entrepreneurship, you can approach your entrepreneurial journey with clarity, confidence, and a realistic understanding of what it takes to succeed. Embrace the challenges, learn from failures, and stay focused on your goals, and you'll be well on your way to entrepreneurial greatness.

~~~~~~~~~~~~~~~~~~~~~~~~~~~~~~~~
~~~~~~~~~~~~~~~~~~~~~~~~~~~~~~~~

Chapter 2: Self-Assessment and Goal Setting

2.1 Assessing Personal Strengths, Skills, and Passions

Before embarking on your entrepreneurial journey, it's essential to conduct a thorough self-assessment to identify your personal strengths, skills, and passions. Understanding what you bring to the table will not only guide your decision-making process but also play a crucial role in shaping your business idea and strategy. In this chapter, we explore effective methods for assessing your strengths, skills, and passions and leveraging them to achieve entrepreneurial success.

Identifying Your Personal Strengths:

1. **Skills and Expertise:** Take inventory of your professional skills, expertise, and areas of knowledge. Identify areas where you excel and consider how you can leverage these skills in your business venture.

2. **Personality Traits:** Reflect on your personality traits, such as leadership abilities, communication skills, and resilience. Recognize how these traits can contribute to your success as an entrepreneur.

3. **Past Experiences:** Consider your past experiences, both personal and professional, and the lessons you've learned along the way. Identify strengths that have emerged from overcoming challenges and achieving successes.

Assessing Your Skills and Expertise:

- **Skills Inventory:** Create a list of your technical skills, soft skills, and specialized knowledge areas. Consider how each skill can be applied in the context of your business venture.
- **Feedback:** Seek feedback from peers, mentors, and colleagues to gain insights into your strengths and areas for improvement. Their perspectives can provide valuable insights into your skills and expertise.

Exploring Your Passions:

1. **Interests and Hobbies:** Consider your interests, hobbies, and passions outside of work. Identify activities that energize and inspire you, as these can provide valuable clues about potential business ideas.

2. **Values and Beliefs:** Reflect on your core values, beliefs, and aspirations. Consider how you can align your business venture with your values and create a meaningful impact in areas that matter to you.

Leveraging Your Personal Strengths, Skills, and Passions:

- **Alignment with Business Idea:** Evaluate how your personal strengths, skills, and passions align with your business idea. Identify opportunities to leverage these assets to differentiate your business and create value for your customers.
- **Continuous Development:** Commit to continuous learning and development to enhance your strengths and skills further. Invest in training, workshops, and

networking opportunities that will help you grow as an entrepreneur.

Assessing your personal strengths, skills, and passions is a crucial step in the entrepreneurial journey. By understanding what you bring to the table and how you can leverage these assets effectively, you can create a solid foundation for building a successful business. Embrace your strengths, pursue your passions, and let your unique abilities guide you towards entrepreneurial greatness.

~~~~~~~~~~~~~~~~~~~~
~~~~~~~~~~~~~~~~~~~~

2.2 Defining Short-term and Long-term Business Goals

Setting clear and actionable goals is essential for driving progress and success in your entrepreneurial journey. In this chapter, we delve into the importance of defining both short-term and long-term business goals and provide practical guidance on how to establish goals that are achievable, measurable, and aligned with your vision for your business.

Understanding Short-term and Long-term Goals:

- **Short-term Goals:** Short-term goals are objectives that you aim to achieve within a relatively brief timeframe, typically ranging from a few weeks to a year. They are essential for keeping you focused and motivated in the short term, as well as for laying the groundwork for your long-term success.

- **Long-term Goals:** Long-term goals, on the other hand, are aspirations that you work towards over an extended period, often spanning several years or even decades. They provide a sense of direction and purpose, guiding your decisions and actions as you navigate the challenges and opportunities of entrepreneurship.

Benefits of Setting Short-term and Long-term Goals:

1. **Clarity and Focus:** Setting goals helps clarify your priorities and focus your efforts on what matters most to your business.

2. **Motivation and Accountability:** Goals provide a source of motivation and accountability, driving you to take consistent action towards achieving your vision.

3. **Measurement and Progress Tracking:** Goals enable you to measure your progress and track your achievements over time, allowing you to celebrate successes and identify areas for improvement.

Defining Short-term Goals:

- **Specific and Measurable:** Set clear and specific objectives that are measurable and quantifiable. Define what success looks like for each goal and establish metrics for tracking progress.

- **Achievable and Realistic:** Ensure that your short-term goals are achievable within the given timeframe and realistic given your resources and constraints. Break down larger goals into smaller, manageable tasks to increase attainability.

- **Time-bound:** Assign deadlines to each short-term goal to create a sense of urgency and accountability. Establish milestones and checkpoints to monitor progress and adjust your approach as needed.

Setting Long-term Goals:

- **Visionary and Inspirational:** Long-term goals should reflect your overarching vision for your business and inspire you to reach new heights of success.

- **Strategic and Aligned:** Align long-term goals with your business strategy and values, ensuring that they contribute to the overall growth and sustainability of your venture.

- **Flexible and Adaptive:** While long-term goals provide a roadmap for your journey, remain flexible and open to adjusting your goals as circumstances change and new opportunities arise.

Defining both short-term and long-term goals is essential for driving progress and success in your entrepreneurial journey. By setting clear, actionable goals that are aligned with your vision and values, you can chart a course towards achieving your dreams and building a thriving business. Embrace the journey, stay focused on your goals, and let your aspirations guide you towards entrepreneurial greatness.

~~~~~~~~~~~~~~~~~~~~~~~~~~~~~
~~~~~~~~~~~~~~~~~~~~~~~~~~~~~

2.3 Creating a Vision Board and Goal Setting Exercise

Visualizing your goals and aspirations is a powerful way to clarify your vision and stay motivated on your entrepreneurial journey. In this chapter, we explore the concept of creating a vision board—a tangible representation of your dreams and goals—and guide you through a goal-setting exercise to translate your vision into actionable objectives.

Understanding the Vision Board: A vision board is a visual representation of your goals, dreams, and aspirations. It serves as a powerful tool for manifesting your desires and keeping you focused on what you want to achieve. By compiling images, words, and symbols that resonate with your vision, you create a visual reminder of your goals that inspires and motivates you to take action.

Steps to Create a Vision Board:

1. **Clarify Your Vision:** Start by clarifying your long-term vision for your business and your life. What do you want to achieve? What does success look like to you? Visualize your ideal future and identify key themes and aspirations.

2. **Gather Inspiration:** Collect images, quotes, and symbols that resonate with your vision and goals. This could include photos, magazine clippings, affirmations, and anything else that inspires you and aligns with your aspirations.

3. **Create Your Vision Board:** Arrange your chosen images and words on a board or poster in a way that

feels meaningful and visually appealing to you. Get creative and use colors, textures, and layouts that reflect your personality and vision.

4. **Display Your Vision Board:** Place your vision board in a prominent location where you'll see it every day—such as your office, bedroom, or workspace. Take time to reflect on your vision board regularly and visualize yourself achieving your goals.

Goal Setting Exercise:

1. **Reflect on Your Vision:** Take a moment to review your vision board and reflect on the goals and aspirations it represents. What specific objectives do you want to achieve based on your vision?

2. **Define Your Goals:** Break down your vision into actionable goals that are specific, measurable, achievable, relevant, and time-bound (SMART). Write down each goal in clear and concise language.

3. **Prioritize Your Goals:** Prioritize your goals based on their importance and urgency. Identify which goals are most critical to achieving your vision and focus your efforts accordingly.

4. **Create Action Plans:** Develop action plans for each goal outlining the steps you need to take to accomplish them. Set deadlines and milestones to track your progress and hold yourself accountable.

Creating a vision board and engaging in goal-setting exercises are powerful tools for clarifying your vision and translating it into actionable objectives. By visualizing your goals and breaking them down into manageable tasks, you can stay focused, motivated, and aligned with your aspirations as you navigate the challenges and opportunities of entrepreneurship. Embrace the process, stay committed to your vision, and let your dreams guide you towards entrepreneurial greatness.

~~~~~~~~~~~~~~~~
~~~~~~~~~~~~~~~~

3.1 Generating Business Ideas and Brainstorming Techniques

Generating innovative business ideas is the cornerstone of entrepreneurship. In this chapter, we explore effective strategies for generating business ideas and introduce brainstorming techniques to spark creativity and uncover opportunities in the market.

Understanding the Ideation Process: The ideation process involves generating, developing, and refining business ideas that have the potential to solve problems, meet market needs, and create value for customers. By embracing creativity, curiosity, and a willingness to explore new possibilities, entrepreneurs can uncover innovative ideas that form the foundation of successful ventures.

Strategies for Generating Business Ideas:

1. **Identify Market Needs:** Start by identifying gaps or pain points in the market where there is unmet demand or room for improvement. Conduct market research, analyze trends, and gather feedback from potential customers to uncover opportunities.

2. **Tap into Your Passion:** Consider your interests, hobbies, and areas of expertise as sources of inspiration for business ideas. Building a business around something you're passionate about can provide intrinsic motivation and increase your chances of success.

3. **Solve Personal Problems:** Reflect on challenges or frustrations you've encountered in your own life and consider how you can develop solutions to address

them. Often, solving a personal problem can lead to business opportunities that resonate with others facing similar challenges.

4. **Explore Emerging Trends:** Keep abreast of emerging trends, technologies, and industries that present opportunities for innovation and disruption. Look for ways to leverage these trends to create unique value propositions and competitive advantages.

Brainstorming Techniques:

1. **Mind Mapping:** Start with a central idea or theme and create a visual map of related concepts, associations, and possibilities. Use branching and clustering to explore connections and generate new ideas.

2. **Reverse Thinking:** Challenge conventional assumptions and flip the problem on its head. Instead of asking "How can we solve this problem?" ask "How can we create this problem?" This shift in perspective can lead to innovative solutions.

3. **SCAMPER Method:** SCAMPER is an acronym that stands for Substitute, Combine, Adapt, Modify, Put to Another Use, Eliminate, and Reverse. Use these prompts to stimulate creativity and explore different ways to innovate and improve existing ideas.

4. **Role Play:** Imagine yourself in the shoes of different stakeholders—such as customers, competitors, or industry experts—and explore the problem from their perspective. This empathetic approach can yield fresh insights and uncover new opportunities.

Generating business ideas is a creative and iterative process that requires curiosity, open-mindedness, and a willingness to explore new possibilities. By tapping into market needs, leveraging personal passions, and embracing innovative brainstorming techniques, entrepreneurs can uncover unique opportunities and develop compelling business concepts that have the potential to thrive in the marketplace. Embrace experimentation, stay open to new ideas, and let your creativity lead the way as you embark on your entrepreneurial journey.

~~~~~~~~~~~~~~~
~~~~~~~~~~~~~~~

3.2 Conducting Market Research and Identifying Target Audience

Market research is a critical step in the entrepreneurial journey, providing valuable insights into customer needs, preferences, and behaviors. In this chapter, we explore the importance of conducting market research and provide guidance on identifying your target audience to inform your business strategy and decision-making process.

Understanding Market Research: Market research involves gathering and analyzing information about the market environment, including industry trends, competitor analysis, and customer insights. By conducting thorough market research, entrepreneurs can make informed decisions, identify opportunities, and mitigate risks associated with launching a new venture.

Key Components of Market Research:

1. **Industry Analysis:** Evaluate the size, growth rate, and dynamics of the industry in which you plan to operate. Identify key players, market trends, and potential barriers to entry that may impact your business.

2. **Competitor Analysis:** Study your competitors to understand their strengths, weaknesses, and market positioning. Identify gaps in the market and opportunities to differentiate your offering.

3. **Customer Insights:** Gain a deep understanding of your target audience's needs, preferences, and purchasing behaviors. Conduct surveys, interviews, and focus groups to gather feedback and validate your business concept.

4. **Market Trends:** Stay abreast of emerging trends, technological advancements, and shifts in consumer behavior that may impact your industry. Anticipate future market needs and position your business accordingly.

Identifying Your Target Audience:

1. **Demographic Characteristics:** Define the demographic profile of your target audience, including age, gender, income level, education, and location. Understanding these demographics will help you tailor your marketing efforts and product offerings.

2. **Psychographic Factors:** Consider the psychographic characteristics of your target audience, such as lifestyle preferences, values, interests, and purchasing motivations. Develop customer personas to segment your audience and personalize your marketing messages.

3. **Behavioral Insights:** Analyze your target audience's purchasing behaviors, buying habits, and decision-making processes. Identify pain points, challenges, and unmet needs that your product or service can address.

4. **Market Segmentation:** Divide your target audience into distinct segments based on common characteristics or behaviors. This allows you to tailor your marketing strategies and product offerings to meet the specific needs of each segment.

Methods for Conducting Market Research:

- **Surveys and Questionnaires:** Gather feedback from potential customers through online surveys, email questionnaires, or in-person interviews.

- **Observational Research:** Observe consumer behavior in real-world settings, such as retail stores or online platforms, to gain insights into their preferences and decision-making processes.

- **Secondary Research:** Utilize existing data and resources, such as industry reports, academic studies, and government statistics, to supplement your primary research efforts.

Conducting market research and identifying your target audience are essential steps in the entrepreneurial journey, providing the foundation for informed decision-making and strategic planning. By gaining insights into industry trends, competitor dynamics, and customer preferences, entrepreneurs can position their businesses for success and create products and services that resonate with their target audience. Embrace the research process, stay curious, and let data-driven insights guide your entrepreneurial endeavors as you navigate the complexities of the marketplace.

~~~~~~~~~~~~~~~~~~~~~~~~~~~~~~~~~~~~~~
~~~~~~~~~~~~~~~~~~~~~~~~~~~~~~~~~~~~~~

3.3 Validating Business Ideas through Surveys and Focus Groups

Validating business ideas is a critical step in the entrepreneurial journey to ensure that your concepts align with market needs and have the potential for success. In this chapter, we explore the process of validating business ideas through surveys and focus groups, enabling entrepreneurs to gather valuable feedback and insights from target customers.

The Importance of Idea Validation: Before investing time, resources, and effort into developing a business idea, it's essential to validate its viability in the market. Idea validation involves gathering feedback from potential customers to assess interest, demand, and willingness to pay for your product or service. By validating your business idea early on, you can mitigate risks, refine your concept, and increase your chances of success.

Surveys for Idea Validation:
1. **Define Objectives:** Start by clearly defining the objectives of your survey. What specific questions do you want to answer? What insights are you seeking to gain from potential customers?

2. **Design Survey Questions:** Develop survey questions that are clear, concise, and focused on gathering actionable feedback. Use a mix of multiple-choice, open-ended, and rating scale questions to capture a range of perspectives.

3. **Select Target Audience:** Identify your target audience and determine the most effective channels for reaching them. Consider using online survey platforms, social media, email lists, or in-person interactions to distribute your survey.

4. **Analyze Results:** Once you've collected survey responses, analyze the data to identify trends, patterns, and insights. Look for common themes, preferences, and pain points that can inform your business strategy and decision-making process.

Focus Groups for Idea Validation:

1. **Recruit Participants:** Identify and recruit a diverse group of participants who represent your target market. Aim for a mix of demographics, backgrounds, and perspectives to ensure a well-rounded discussion.

2. **Facilitate Discussion:** Plan and facilitate a structured focus group session to explore participants' opinions, attitudes, and preferences regarding your business idea. Encourage open and honest dialogue while maintaining a neutral stance as the moderator.

3. **Capture Insights:** Take detailed notes during the focus group session to capture key insights, observations, and feedback from participants. Pay attention to both verbal and non-verbal cues to uncover valuable insights.

4. **Debrief and Analyze:** After the focus group, debrief with your team to discuss and analyze the feedback received. Identify common themes, areas of consensus, and areas for further exploration or refinement.

Validating business ideas through surveys and focus groups is a critical step in the entrepreneurial process to ensure that your concepts resonate with target customers and address real market needs. By gathering feedback early on and incorporating it into your business strategy, you can increase the likelihood of success and build a solid foundation for your venture. Embrace the validation process, listen to your customers, and use their insights to refine and improve your business ideas as you progress on your entrepreneurial journey.

~~~~~~~~~~~~~~~~~~~~~~~~~~~~~~~~~~~~~
~~~~~~~~~~~~~~~~~~~~~~~~~~~~~~~~~~~~~

Part II: Planning Your Business

4.1 Importance of a Business Plan

A business plan serves as a roadmap for your entrepreneurial journey, providing a strategic framework to guide your decisions and actions as you build and grow your venture. In this chapter, we explore the importance of a business plan and how it contributes to the success of your business.

1. Clarifies Your Vision:

- A business plan helps clarify your vision for your business by defining your goals, objectives, and strategies. It articulates your mission statement, core values, and long-term vision, providing a clear direction for your venture.

2. Sets Clear Objectives:

- By outlining specific and measurable objectives, a business plan helps you set clear milestones and targets to track your progress. It establishes timelines, deadlines, and performance metrics to keep you accountable and focused on achieving your goals.

3. Attracts Investors and Funding:

- A well-developed business plan is essential for attracting investors, lenders, and other stakeholders who may provide funding or support for your business. It demonstrates your understanding of the market, your competitive advantage, and your potential for profitability.

4. Guides Decision-Making:

- A business plan serves as a reference point for making informed decisions about your business. It provides a framework for evaluating opportunities, assessing risks, and prioritizing initiatives, ensuring that your decisions align with your overall strategy.

5. Identifies Strengths and Weaknesses:

- Through market analysis, competitive research, and financial projections, a business plan helps you identify the strengths and weaknesses of your business. It enables you to capitalize on opportunities and mitigate potential threats in the marketplace.

6. Facilitates Communication and Collaboration:

- A business plan serves as a communication tool for sharing your vision and strategy with key stakeholders, including employees, partners, and suppliers. It fosters collaboration and alignment across your organization, ensuring everyone is working towards common goals.

7. Provides a Roadmap for Growth:

- As your business evolves, a business plan provides a roadmap for growth and expansion. It outlines strategies for scaling your operations, entering new markets, and diversifying your product or service offerings, enabling you to adapt to changing market conditions.

8. Enhances Accountability:

- By documenting your goals, strategies, and action plans, a business plan enhances accountability within your organization. It provides a basis for measuring performance, tracking results, and holding yourself and your team accountable for achieving objectives.

A business plan is a foundational document that plays a critical role in the success of your business. By clarifying your vision, setting clear objectives, attracting investors, guiding decision-making, identifying strengths and weaknesses, facilitating communication, providing a roadmap for growth, and enhancing accountability, a business plan serves as a blueprint for building a thriving and sustainable venture. Embrace the process of business planning and leverage your plan as a strategic tool to navigate the complexities of entrepreneurship and achieve your goals.

~~~~~~~~~~~~~~~~~~~~~~~~~
~~~~~~~~~~~~~~~~~~~~~~~~~

4.2 Components of a Comprehensive Business Plan

A comprehensive business plan serves as a blueprint for your entrepreneurial journey, outlining key aspects of your business and providing a strategic roadmap for success. In this chapter, we explore the essential components of a comprehensive business plan and their significance in guiding your venture.

1. Executive Summary: The executive summary provides an overview of your business plan, highlighting key elements such as your business concept, target market, competitive advantage, and financial projections. It serves as a snapshot of your entire plan and should capture the reader's attention and interest.

2. Business Description: The business description section provides detailed information about your business concept, including your mission statement, vision, and core values. It outlines the nature of your business, your products or services, and your unique value proposition.

3. Market Analysis: The market analysis section evaluates the industry landscape, target market demographics, customer needs and preferences, and competitive landscape. It identifies market trends, opportunities, and challenges, helping you understand your market positioning and potential for success.

4. Marketing and Sales Strategy: The marketing and sales strategy outlines how you plan to attract and retain customers, promote your products or services, and generate revenue. It includes details about your pricing strategy, distribution channels, advertising and promotional tactics, and sales forecasts.

5. Operational Plan: The operational plan describes the day-to-day operations of your business, including your organizational structure, staffing requirements, facilities and equipment, and operational processes. It outlines how you will produce and deliver your products or services efficiently and effectively.

6. Financial Plan: The financial plan presents your business's financial projections, including income statements, cash flow forecasts, and balance sheets. It outlines your startup costs, revenue projections, expenses, break-even analysis, and funding requirements, providing a roadmap for financial sustainability and growth.

7. Management and Organization: The management and organization section introduces key members of your management team and provides an overview of their roles, responsibilities, and qualifications. It also outlines your organizational structure, governance, and legal structure.

8. Implementation Plan: The implementation plan outlines the steps and timelines for executing your business plan and achieving your goals. It breaks down your strategies and action plans into actionable tasks, assigns responsibilities, and establishes milestones and deadlines for tracking progress.

A comprehensive business plan consists of several essential components that collectively provide a roadmap for building and growing your business. By addressing each component thoroughly and thoughtfully, you can ensure that your business plan effectively communicates your vision, strategies, and goals to stakeholders and guides your entrepreneurial journey towards success. Embrace the process of developing a comprehensive business plan and leverage it as a strategic tool to navigate the complexities of entrepreneurship and achieve your aspirations.

~~~~~~~~~~~~~~~~~~~~~~~~~~~~~~~~~~~~
~~~~~~~~~~~~~~~~~~~~~~~~~~~~~~~~~~~~

4.3 Writing an Executive Summary and Company Description

The executive summary and company description are critical components of a business plan, providing a concise overview of your venture and setting the stage for the rest of the document. In this section, we delve into the importance of crafting an effective executive summary and company description and provide guidance on how to do so.

1. Executive Summary: The executive summary serves as the introduction to your business plan, capturing the reader's attention and providing a snapshot of your venture's key elements. It should concisely summarize the most important aspects of your business plan and compel the reader to continue reading. Key components of an effective executive summary include:

- **Business Concept:** Briefly describe your business concept, including your products or services, target market, and unique value proposition.

- **Market Opportunity:** Highlight the market opportunity you are addressing and provide an overview of the industry landscape, market trends, and competitive environment.

- **Financial Highlights:** Summarize your financial projections, including revenue forecasts, startup costs, and funding requirements.

- **Key Achievements and Milestones:** Highlight any significant achievements, milestones, or traction your business has achieved to date, such as partnerships, customer testimonials, or product development milestones.

- **Call to Action:** Conclude the executive summary with a call to action, such as requesting funding, inviting further discussion, or outlining next steps.

2. Company Description: The company description provides an in-depth overview of your business, detailing its mission, vision, values, and core capabilities. It sets the stage for the rest of the business plan by providing context and background information about your venture. Key components of a comprehensive company description include:

- **Mission and Vision:** Articulate your company's mission and vision statements, outlining its purpose, goals, and aspirations.

- **Core Values:** Identify the core values that guide your business operations and shape its culture and identity.

- **Business Model:** Describe your business model, including how you create, deliver, and capture value for your customers.

- **Market Opportunity:** Provide insights into the market opportunity you are pursuing, including the size of the market, target demographics, and customer needs.

- **Competitive Advantage:** Highlight your competitive advantage, such as unique features, proprietary technology, or strategic partnerships, that set your business apart from competitors.

Crafting a compelling executive summary and company description is essential for effectively communicating your business concept, vision, and value proposition to stakeholders. By succinctly summarizing the most critical aspects of your venture and providing context and background information, you can capture the reader's interest and set the stage for a thorough exploration of your business plan. Embrace the opportunity to showcase the uniqueness and potential of your venture through a well-crafted executive summary and company description.

~~~~~~~~~~~~~~~~~~~~~~~~~~~~~~~~~~~~~
~~~~~~~~~~~~~~~~~~~~~~~~~~~~~~~~~~~~~

Chapter 5: Legal and Regulatory Considerations

5.1 Choosing the Right Legal Structure for Your Business

Selecting the appropriate legal structure for your business is a crucial decision that can impact various aspects of your venture, including liability, taxation, and operational flexibility. In this chapter, we explore the different legal structures available to entrepreneurs and provide guidance on choosing the right one for your business.

1. Sole Proprietorship:
- **Overview:** A sole proprietorship is the simplest form of business structure, where the business is owned and operated by a single individual. The owner is personally liable for all debts and obligations of the business.

- **Advantages:** Easy and inexpensive to set up, complete control over decision-making, and minimal regulatory requirements.

- **Disadvantages:** Unlimited personal liability, limited access to financing, and potential challenges in scaling the business.

2. Partnership:
- **Overview:** A partnership is formed when two or more individuals share ownership and management responsibilities of a business. Partners share profits, losses, and liabilities according to the terms of a partnership agreement.

- **Advantages:** Shared decision-making and resources, flexibility in management structure, and potential tax benefits.

- **Disadvantages:** Unlimited liability for general partners, potential conflicts between partners, and challenges in resolving disputes.

3. Limited Liability Company (LLC):

- **Overview:** An LLC combines the limited liability protection of a corporation with the flexibility and tax advantages of a partnership. Owners, known as members, are not personally liable for the debts and obligations of the business.

- **Advantages:** Limited liability protection, flexible management structure, pass-through taxation, and minimal regulatory requirements.

- **Disadvantages:** Formation and administrative costs, potential complexity in management and governance, and variations in state regulations.

4. Corporation:

- **Overview:** A corporation is a separate legal entity that is owned by shareholders and managed by a board of directors. Shareholders enjoy limited liability protection, and the corporation can raise capital through the issuance of stock.

- **Advantages:** Limited liability protection for shareholders, access to capital markets, perpetual existence, and potential tax advantages.

- **Disadvantages:** Complex formation and compliance requirements, double taxation of profits, and stringent regulatory oversight.

5. Private Limited Company:

- **Overview:** A private limited company is a legal entity separate from its owners, offering limited liability protection to shareholders and enabling the issuance of shares to a restricted group of individuals. It combines the benefits of a corporation with the flexibility of a partnership.

- **Advantages:** Limited liability protection for shareholders, separate legal entity status, access to capital through share issuance, and enhanced credibility with stakeholders.

- **Disadvantages:** Compliance requirements, regulatory oversight, and restrictions on transferability of shares.

6. Nonprofit Organization:

- **Overview:** A nonprofit organization is formed for purposes other than generating profit, such as charitable, educational, or religious activities. It operates similarly to a corporation but is subject to specific regulations governing nonprofit entities.

- **Advantages:** Tax-exempt status, eligibility for grants and donations, and the ability to pursue social or charitable missions.

- **Disadvantages:** Restrictions on profit distribution, compliance with regulatory requirements, and limitations on activities and fundraising.

Choosing the Right Legal Structure:

- **Consider Your Business Needs:** Evaluate your business goals, growth plans, and risk tolerance to determine the most suitable legal structure.

- **Consult with Legal and Financial Advisors:** Seek guidance from legal and financial professionals who can provide insights into the legal, tax, and financial implications of different business structures.

- **Review Regulatory Requirements:** Familiarize yourself with the legal and regulatory requirements associated with each legal structure, including formation, reporting, and compliance obligations.

- **Assess Liability and Tax Implications:** Consider the level of personal liability protection and the tax implications of each legal structure, taking into account your risk exposure and tax efficiency goals.

Choosing the right legal structure for your business is a critical decision that requires careful consideration of various factors, including liability, taxation, and operational flexibility. By understanding the characteristics and implications of different legal structures, seeking professional advice, and aligning your choice with your business goals and objectives, you can establish a solid foundation for your venture and navigate the complexities of legal and regulatory compliance with confidence. Embrace the opportunity to structure your business in a way that maximizes benefits and minimizes risks, setting the stage for long-term success and sustainability.

~~~~~~
~~~~~~

5.2 Understanding Business Registration and Licensing Requirements

Navigating the legal and regulatory landscape is essential for any business to operate smoothly and compliantly. In this chapter, we delve into the importance of understanding business registration and licensing requirements and provide guidance on the steps entrepreneurs need to take to ensure legal compliance.

1. Business Registration:

- **Overview:** Business registration is the process of officially establishing your business as a legal entity with the relevant government authorities. It grants your business legal recognition and enables you to operate within the bounds of the law.

- **Types of Business Entities:** Depending on your business structure, registration requirements may vary. Common types of business entities include sole proprietorships, partnerships, private limited (Pvt. Ltd.), limited liability companies (LLCs), corporations, and nonprofit organizations.

- **Registration Process:** The registration process typically involves submitting necessary documentation, such as articles of incorporation, partnership agreements, or registration forms, along with applicable fees, to the appropriate government agency. The specific requirements vary by jurisdiction and business structure.

2. Licensing Requirements:

- **Overview:** In addition to business registration, many businesses require specific licenses or permits to operate legally in their industry or locality. These licenses may be issued by federal, state, or local government agencies and are designed to ensure public safety, health, and welfare.

- **Types of Licenses:** Licensing requirements vary depending on the nature of your business and the industry in which you operate. Common types of licenses include business licenses, professional licenses, health permits, zoning permits, and environmental permits.

- **Research and Compliance:** Before launching your business, it's essential to research and identify the specific licenses and permits required for your industry and location. Failure to obtain necessary licenses can result in fines, penalties, or even the closure of your business.

3. Regulatory Compliance:

- **Overview:** Regulatory compliance refers to the process of ensuring that your business operations adhere to relevant laws, regulations, and industry standards. Compliance is essential for protecting your business, employees, customers, and stakeholders and avoiding legal liabilities.

- **Areas of Compliance:** Regulatory requirements may encompass various areas, including labor and employment laws, taxation, health and safety regulations, environmental regulations, data protection and privacy laws, and industry-specific regulations.

- **Stay Informed and Updated:** As regulations and laws are subject to change, it's crucial to stay informed about developments that may impact on your business. Regularly review regulatory updates, seek legal counsel when necessary, and establish internal processes to ensure ongoing compliance.

4. Consultation and Legal Advice:

- **Seek Professional Guidance:** Navigating business registration and licensing requirements can be complex, especially for new entrepreneurs. Consider seeking assistance from legal advisors, business consultants, or industry associations who can provide guidance and support throughout the process.

- **Due Diligence:** Conduct thorough due diligence to ensure that you understand all legal obligations and requirements associated with your business. Taking proactive steps to address compliance issues can help mitigate risks and set the stage for long-term success.

Understanding business registration and licensing is essential for legal compliance. Familiarize yourself with the registration process, obtain necessary licenses, ensure regulatory compliance, and seek professional guidance. This will help you navigate the legal landscape confidently, setting your business up for long-term success and growth. Embrace this opportunity to build a strong foundation for your venture.

5.3 Compliance with Taxation Laws and Regulatory Obligations

Ensuring compliance with taxation laws and regulatory obligations is paramount for the success and sustainability of any business. In this chapter, we explore the importance of compliance with taxation laws and regulatory obligations and provide guidance on how entrepreneurs can navigate these complex legal requirements.

1. Understanding Taxation Laws:

- **Tax Obligations:** Businesses are subject to various taxes, including income tax, sales tax, payroll tax, property tax, and excise tax, among others. Understanding your tax obligations is essential for avoiding penalties and maintaining financial health.

- **Tax Planning:** Effective tax planning can help minimize tax liabilities while maximizing available deductions and credits. Consider consulting with tax professionals to develop a tax strategy tailored to your business needs and goals.

2. Registering for Tax Identification Numbers:

- **Employer Identification Number (EIN):** Most businesses are required to obtain an Employer Identification Number (EIN) from the Internal Revenue Service (IRS). An EIN is used to identify your business for tax purposes and is necessary for hiring employees, opening bank accounts, and filing tax returns.

- **State Tax IDs:** Depending on your location and business activities, you may also need to register for state tax identification numbers for sales tax, withholding tax, or other state-specific taxes.

3. Maintaining Accurate Financial Records:

- **Record-Keeping Requirements:** Businesses are required to maintain accurate and up-to-date financial records, including income statements, balance sheets, cash flow statements, and supporting documentation for expenses and deductions.

- **Accounting Systems:** Implementing robust accounting systems and practices can streamline record-keeping processes and ensure compliance with regulatory reporting requirements.

4. Filing Tax Returns and Payments:

- **Tax Filing Deadlines:** Familiarize yourself with tax filing deadlines for federal, state, and local taxes, including income tax returns, sales tax returns, and payroll tax returns. Missing deadlines can result in penalties and interest charges.

- **Estimated Taxes:** If your business expects to owe a significant amount of taxes, you may be required to make estimated tax payments throughout the year to avoid underpayment penalties.

5. Compliance with Regulatory Obligations:

- **Industry-Specific Regulations:** Depending on your industry, your business may be subject to specific regulatory requirements and compliance obligations. Examples include health and safety regulations, environmental regulations, data protection laws, and licensing requirements.

- **Monitoring Regulatory Changes:** Stay informed about changes to tax laws and regulations that may affect your business. Regularly review updates from tax authorities and seek professional advice to ensure ongoing compliance.

6. Seek Professional Guidance:

- **Tax Advisors and Consultants:** Consider working with tax advisors, accountants, or consultants who specialize in business taxation. They can provide guidance on tax planning strategies, assist with tax return preparation, and help address any compliance issues that arise.

- **Legal Counsel:** In complex tax matters or regulatory compliance issues, seek legal counsel from experienced attorneys who can provide expert advice and representation. Investing in professional guidance can help mitigate risks and ensure that your business operates within the bounds of the law.

Compliance with taxation laws and regulatory obligations is essential for establishing a strong business foundation and avoiding legal and financial consequences. Understand your tax obligations, register for necessary IDs, maintain accurate records, file returns on time, stay informed about regulatory changes, and seek professional guidance. This proactive approach will help you build a compliant, sustainable business that thrives in today's regulatory environment.

~~~~~~
~~~~~~

6.1 Estimating Startup Costs and Initial Investment

Before launching your business, it's essential to estimate the startup costs and initial investment required to get your venture off the ground. In this chapter, we explore the process of estimating startup costs and initial investment and provide guidance on how to budget effectively for your business launch.

1. Identifying Startup Costs:

- **One-Time Expenses:** Startup costs typically include one-time expenses incurred before your business begins generating revenue. These may include costs for equipment, furniture, inventory, leasehold improvements, legal fees, permits, licenses, and initial marketing expenses.

- **Ongoing Expenses:** In addition to one-time expenses, consider ongoing operational costs such as rent, utilities, salaries, insurance, marketing, and inventory replenishment. These expenses will continue to be incurred as your business operates.

2. Creating a Startup Cost Checklist:

- **Comprehensive List:** Develop a comprehensive checklist of all potential startup costs, categorizing them into one-time and ongoing expenses. This will help ensure that you capture all necessary costs and avoid surprises later on.

- **Research and Quotes:** Research costs associated with each item on your checklist and obtain quotes from vendors, suppliers, and service providers. Be thorough in your research to accurately estimate costs and avoid underestimating expenses.

3. Estimating Initial Investment:

- **Total Funding Needed:** Once you've identified all startup costs, calculate the total funding needed to launch your business. This will include both initial investment and working capital to cover ongoing expenses until your business becomes profitable.

- **Contingency Fund:** It's wise to include a contingency fund in your initial investment to account for unexpected expenses or fluctuations in revenue. A contingency fund provides a buffer against unforeseen challenges and ensures that you have sufficient resources to weather potential setbacks.

4. Sources of Funding:

- **Personal Savings:** Many entrepreneurs use personal savings to fund the initial investment in their business. This may include savings accumulated over time, retirement funds, or proceeds from the sale of assets.

- **External Financing:** Depending on the scale of your business and your funding needs, you may consider external sources of financing such as bank loans, lines of credit, venture capital, angel investors, crowdfunding, or grants.

- **Bootstrapping:** Bootstrapping involves funding your business through revenue generated from sales rather than relying on external financing. While bootstrapping requires careful budgeting and resourcefulness, it allows you to maintain control and avoid debt.

5. Developing a Financial Plan:

- **Budgeting:** Develop a detailed financial plan that outlines your projected income, expenses, and cash flow for the first year of operation. Use realistic estimates based on market research, industry benchmarks, and historical data where available.

- **Cash Flow Management:** Effective cash flow management is critical for ensuring that your business has sufficient liquidity to meet its financial obligations. Monitor your cash flow regularly and implement strategies to optimize cash flow, such as managing accounts receivable and accounts payable.

Estimating startup costs and initial investment is a crucial step in the business planning process, setting the foundation for a successful launch and sustainable growth. By identifying all startup costs, creating a comprehensive checklist, estimating the total funding needed, exploring sources of funding, and developing a financial plan, you can effectively budget for your business launch and mitigate financial risks. Embrace the opportunity to plan and budget strategically, laying the groundwork for a resilient and financially sound business that thrives in today's competitive landscape.

6.2 Creating a Business Budget and Cash Flow Forecast

A well-defined budget and cash flow forecast are essential tools for managing the financial aspects of your business effectively. In this chapter, we delve into the process of creating a business budget and cash flow forecast and provide guidance on how to develop these critical financial documents.

1. Importance of a Business Budget:

- **Financial Roadmap:** A business budget serves as a financial roadmap, outlining your anticipated income and expenses over a specific period, typically one year. It provides a clear overview of your financial situation and helps you make informed decisions about resource allocation and investment priorities.

- **Control and Accountability:** By establishing a budget, you gain greater control over your finances and hold yourself accountable for adhering to spending limits and financial targets. A budget allows you to track your progress, identify variances, and take corrective action as needed to stay on course.

2. Components of a Business Budget:

- **Revenue Projections:** Estimate your expected revenue based on sales forecasts, pricing strategies, and market demand. Consider different revenue streams and growth opportunities to create a realistic revenue projection.

- **Operating Expenses:** Identify and categorize all operating expenses, including rent, utilities, salaries, marketing, supplies, insurance, and maintenance. Be thorough in capturing all potential expenses to ensure an accurate budget.
- **Capital Expenditures:** Factor in any capital expenditures or one-time investments required to support your business operations, such as equipment purchases, facility upgrades, or technology investments.

3. Developing a Cash Flow Forecast:

- **Cash Inflows:** Project your expected cash inflows from sales, investments, loans, and other sources. Consider the timing of cash receipts and account for seasonality or cyclical fluctuations in your business.

- **Cash Outflows:** Estimate your anticipated cash outflows for operating expenses, loan repayments, taxes, and other financial obligations. Be mindful of timing differences between when expenses are incurred and when payments are due.

- **Managing Cash Flow Gaps:** Identify potential cash flow gaps where cash inflows may not cover outflows. Develop strategies to manage these gaps, such as securing a line of credit, negotiating extended payment terms with suppliers, or accelerating accounts receivable collections.

4. Reviewing and Monitoring Performance:

- **Regular Review:** Review your budget and cash flow forecast regularly to track actual performance against projected figures. Compare actual results to budgeted amounts and analyze variances to understand the reasons behind deviations.

- **Adjustments and Revisions:** Be flexible in your approach and willing to adjust your budget and forecast as circumstances change. Use insights gained from ongoing monitoring to refine your financial projections and improve accuracy over time.

5. Leveraging Financial Tools and Software:

- **Budgeting Software:** Consider using budgeting software or financial management tools to streamline the budgeting process and facilitate ongoing monitoring and analysis. These tools can automate calculations, generate reports, and provide insights to support decision-making.

- **Professional Assistance:** If budgeting and financial forecasting seem daunting, don't hesitate to seek assistance from financial advisors, accountants, or business consultants who can provide guidance and expertise to help you develop robust financial plans.

Creating a business budget and cash flow forecast are essential steps in the financial planning process, enabling you to manage your resources effectively and make informed decisions about resource allocation and investment priorities. By developing a comprehensive budget that accurately reflects your expected revenue, expenses, and cash flow, and regularly monitoring performance against projections, you can maintain financial control and position your business for long-term success and sustainability. Embrace the opportunity to harness the power of financial planning and budgeting to drive growth and prosperity for your business.

~~~~~~
~~~~~~

6.3 Exploring Funding Options and Financing Strategies

Securing adequate funding is essential for launching and growing your business. In this chapter, we explore various funding options and financing strategies available to entrepreneurs, empowering you to make informed decisions about financing your venture.

1. Self-Funding:

- **Personal Savings:** Utilizing personal savings is a common way to fund a new business. It allows you to maintain full control over your venture and eliminates the need to repay external debts. However, it may require significant personal financial investment and involve higher risk.

- **Bootstrapping:** Bootstrapping involves funding your business through revenue generated from sales rather than relying on external financing. While bootstrapping requires careful budgeting and resourcefulness, it enables you to maintain independence and retain ownership.

2. Debt Financing:

- **Bank Loans:** Traditional bank loans are a common form of debt financing, offering fixed or variable interest rates and structured repayment schedules. To qualify for a bank loan, you may need to provide collateral and demonstrate your ability to repay the loan through a solid business plan and financial projections.

- **Lines of Credit:** A line of credit provides flexible access to funds that can be drawn upon as needed. It offers greater flexibility than traditional loans, allowing you to borrow only what you need and repay it on a revolving basis.

3. Equity Financing:

- **Angel Investors:** Angel investors are affluent individuals who provide capital to startups in exchange for ownership equity or convertible debt. They often bring industry expertise and valuable connections in addition to financial investment.

- **Venture Capital:** Venture capital firms invest in high-growth startups with the potential for significant returns. In exchange for funding, they typically require equity ownership and may exert influence over business decisions.

4. Crowdfunding:

- **Reward-Based Crowdfunding:** Platforms such as Kickstarter and Indiegogo allow entrepreneurs to raise funds by offering rewards or pre-sales of products or services to backers. This approach enables you to validate market demand and generate early revenue.

- **Equity Crowdfunding:** Equity crowdfunding platforms enable entrepreneurs to raise capital by selling shares or ownership stakes in their businesses to a large number of investors. It offers the opportunity to access funding from a broad pool of investors without relinquishing control over a single entity.

5. Grants and Subsidies:

- **Government Grants:** Many governments offer grants and subsidies to support small businesses and startups, particularly in sectors such as technology, innovation, and social enterprise. These grants can provide non-dilutive funding without requiring repayment.

- **Industry-Specific Grants:** Some industries and sectors offer specific grants and funding programs to support research, development, and innovation. Explore opportunities within your industry to access additional funding sources.

6. Strategic Partnerships and Joint Ventures:

- **Collaborative Ventures:** Strategic partnerships and joint ventures allow businesses to pool resources, expertise, and networks to pursue shared objectives. By partnering with complementary businesses or organizations, you can access additional funding and expand market reach.

- **Strategic Investors:** Strategic investors, such as corporate partners or industry leaders, may provide capital investment in exchange for strategic benefits, such as access to technology, distribution channels, or market insights.

Explore diverse funding sources like self-funding, debt, equity, crowdfunding, grants, and partnerships. Align your financing approach with goals and adopt creative strategies for sustainable growth in today's dynamic business landscape.

7.1 Developing a Unique Brand Identity and Value Proposition

Creating a distinctive brand identity and value proposition is essential for capturing the attention of your target audience and differentiating your business from competitors. In this chapter, we explore the process of developing a unique brand identity and value proposition that resonates with your customers and drives business success.

1. Understanding Brand Identity:

- **Brand Essence:** Define the core attributes and values that define your brand. Consider what sets your business apart from competitors and how you want to be perceived by customers.

- **Brand Elements:** Develop visual elements such as logos, colors, typography, and imagery that reflect your brand's personality and resonate with your target audience.

2. Crafting a Compelling Value Proposition:

- **Identify Customer Needs:** Understand the needs, desires, and pain points of your target audience. Conduct market research to gain insights into customer preferences and behaviors.

- **Unique Selling Proposition (USP):** Articulate what makes your product or service unique and why customers should choose your brand over alternatives. Focus on the benefits and value you offer that competitors cannot replicate.

3. Brand Messaging and Communication:

- **Brand Storytelling:** Develop a compelling narrative that communicates your brand's story, mission, and values. Use storytelling to connect with customers on an emotional level and build brand affinity.

- **Consistent Messaging:** Ensure consistency in your brand messaging across all touchpoints, including your website, social media, advertising, and customer interactions. Consistent messaging reinforces brand identity and fosters brand recognition.

4. Visual Brand Identity:

- **Logo Design:** Create a visually appealing and memorable logo that represents your brand identity and resonates with your target audience. Your logo should be versatile and scalable, suitable for use across various marketing materials and platforms.

- **Brand Style Guide:** Develop a brand style guide that outlines guidelines for visual elements such as colors, typography, imagery, and design principles. A style guide ensures consistency in brand presentation and reinforces brand recognition.

5. Brand Experience and Customer Engagement:

- **Customer Journey Mapping:** Map out the customer journey to identify key touchpoints and opportunities for interaction with your brand. Focus on delivering a seamless and memorable experience at every stage of the customer lifecycle.

- **Brand Advocacy:** Cultivate brand advocates who are passionate about your brand and willing to advocate on your behalf. Encourage customer feedback, engage with your audience on social media, and foster a sense of community around your brand.

6. Monitoring and Adaptation:

- **Brand Performance Metrics:** Establish key performance indicators (KPIs) to measure the effectiveness of your branding efforts. Monitor metrics such as brand awareness, brand perception, customer engagement, and brand loyalty.
- **Continuous Improvement:** Regularly assess and refine your brand identity and value proposition based on customer feedback, market trends, and competitive analysis. Adapt your branding strategy to evolving market dynamics and emerging opportunities.

Developing a unique brand identity and value proposition is a foundational step in building a successful and enduring business. By understanding your brand essence, crafting a compelling value proposition, communicating effectively with your target audience, and delivering a consistent brand experience, you can create meaningful connections with customers and drive business growth. Embrace the opportunity to differentiate your brand in the marketplace and build a loyal customer base that resonates with your brand's values and vision.

~~~~~~~~~~~~~~~~~~~~~~~~~~~~~~~~~~~~~~
~~~~~~~~~~~~~~~~~~~~~~~~~~~~~~~~~~~~~~

7.2 Crafting a Marketing Plan and Targeting Marketing Channels

A well-defined marketing plan is essential for reaching your target audience, promoting your brand, and driving business growth. In this chapter, we explore the process of crafting a comprehensive marketing plan and selecting the most effective marketing channels to reach your target market.

1. Market Analysis and Segmentation:
- **Identify Target Audience:** Conduct market research to identify your target audience and understand their demographics, preferences, and behaviors. Segment your target market based on factors such as age, gender, income, location, and psychographics.

- **Competitive Analysis:** Analyze competitors' marketing strategies, strengths, and weaknesses to identify opportunities for differentiation and competitive advantage.

2. Setting Marketing Objectives:
- **SMART Goals:** Establish specific, measurable, achievable, relevant, and time-bound (SMART) marketing objectives that align with your overall business goals. Examples include increasing brand awareness, generating leads, driving website traffic, or boosting sales.

3. Developing Marketing Strategies:
- **Brand Positioning:** Define your brand's unique value proposition and positioning in the market.

Determine how you want your brand to be perceived by customers and develop strategies to communicate your brand's value effectively.

- **Marketing Mix:** Develop strategies for the four Ps of marketing—product, price, place, and promotion—to achieve your marketing objectives. Consider factors such as product features, pricing strategies, distribution channels, and promotional tactics.

4. Selecting Marketing Channels:

- **Digital Marketing Channels:** Explore a variety of digital marketing channels, including search engine optimization (SEO), pay-per-click (PPC) advertising, social media marketing, email marketing, content marketing, and influencer marketing. Choose channels that align with your target audience's online behavior and preferences.

- **Traditional Marketing Channels:** Consider traditional marketing channels such as print advertising, television, radio, direct mail, and outdoor advertising, depending on your target market and industry. Evaluate the effectiveness of each channel in reaching and engaging your audience.

5. Creating a Marketing Budget:

- **Allocate Resources:** Determine the financial resources available for marketing activities and allocate budget accordingly. Consider factors such as expected return on investment (ROI), cost-effectiveness of marketing channels, and long-term growth objectives.

- **Budget Allocation:** Allocate budget across different marketing initiatives based on their strategic importance, potential impact, and expected outcomes. Monitor spending and adjust budget allocation as needed to optimize performance and achieve marketing objectives.

6. Implementation and Evaluation:

- **Execution Plan:** Develop a detailed implementation plan outlining the specific actions, timelines, and responsibilities for executing your marketing strategies. Monitor progress and make adjustments as needed to stay on track.

- **Performance Measurement:** Establish key performance indicators (KPIs) to measure the effectiveness of your marketing efforts. Track metrics such as website traffic, lead generation, conversion rates, customer acquisition cost (CAC), and return on investment (ROI).

Crafting a marketing plan and targeting the right marketing channels are essential steps in effectively promoting your brand and reaching your target audience. By conducting market analysis, setting clear marketing objectives, developing strategic marketing strategies, selecting appropriate marketing channels, allocating resources wisely, and monitoring performance, you can create a roadmap for success and drive business growth through effective marketing efforts. Embrace the opportunity to engage with your audience, build brand awareness, and drive customer acquisition by leveraging the power of strategic marketing planning and execution.

~~~~~~~~~~~~~~~~~~~~~~~~~
~~~~~~~~~~~~~~~~~~~~~~~~~

7.3 Building an Online Presence through Website and Social Media

Establishing a strong online presence is essential for modern businesses to connect with their target audience and drive engagement. In this chapter, we explore strategies for building an effective online presence through website development and social media marketing.

1. Website Development:

- **Strategic Planning:** Begin by defining the purpose and objectives of your website. Determine what actions you want visitors to take, such as making a purchase, signing up for a newsletter, or contacting your business.

- **User Experience (UX) Design:** Design your website with the user in mind, focusing on intuitive navigation, clear messaging, and responsive design that adapts to various devices and screen sizes.

- **Content Creation:** Develop high-quality content that provides value to your audience and reflects your brand's personality and expertise. Include informative product descriptions, engaging blog posts, customer testimonials, and visually appealing images or videos.

2. Search Engine Optimization (SEO):

- **Keyword Research:** Identify relevant keywords and phrases that your target audience is likely to use when searching for products or services related to your business. Incorporate these keywords strategically into your website content to improve search engine visibility.

- **On-Page Optimization:** Optimize on-page elements such as title tags, meta descriptions, headings, and image alt text to make your website more search engine friendly and increase organic traffic.

- **Link Building:** Build quality backlinks from reputable websites to improve your website's authority and credibility in the eyes of search engines. Focus on earning links naturally through content creation, guest blogging, and outreach to industry influencers.

3. Social Media Marketing:

- **Platform Selection:** Identify the social media platforms that are most relevant to your target audience and industry. Popular platforms include Facebook, Instagram, Twitter, LinkedIn, Pinterest, and YouTube.

- **Content Strategy:** Develop a content strategy that aligns with your brand identity and resonates with your target audience. Create a mix of content types, including informative articles, engaging visuals, videos, polls, contests, and user-generated content.

- **Community Engagement:** Foster meaningful interactions with your audience by responding to comments, messages, and mentions promptly. Encourage user-generated content, such as customer reviews, testimonials, and user-generated photos or videos, to build community and brand advocacy.

4. Paid Advertising:
- **Social Media Ads:** Leverage paid advertising options offered by social media platforms to reach a larger audience and drive targeted traffic to your website. Experiment with different ad formats, targeting options, and bidding strategies to optimize campaign performance.

- **Search Engine Ads:** Consider running pay-per-click (PPC) advertising campaigns on search engines like Google or Bing to increase visibility for relevant keywords and capture high-intent traffic. Monitor ad performance closely and adjust bidding strategies and ad copy to maximize return on investment (ROI).

5. Performance Tracking and Analysis:
- **Website Analytics:** Use web analytics tools such as Google Analytics to track key metrics such as website traffic, user engagement, conversion rates, and goal completions. Analyze data regularly to identify areas for improvement and optimize website performance.

- **Social Media Insights:** Monitor social media metrics such as reach, engagement, follower growth, and conversion rates to evaluate the effectiveness of your social media efforts. Use insights to refine your content strategy, audience targeting, and advertising tactics.

Building an online presence through website development and social media marketing is essential for businesses to reach and engage their target audience in today's digital landscape. By investing in strategic website development, optimizing for search engines, leveraging social media platforms effectively, and monitoring performance closely, you can establish a strong online presence that drives brand awareness, customer engagement, and business growth. Embrace the opportunity to connect with your audience, build relationships, and expand your online reach through thoughtful and strategic online presence-building initiatives.

~~~~~~
~~~~~~

Part III: Setting Up Your Business

~~~~~~~~~~~~~~~~~~~~~~~~~~~~~~~~~~~~~~~
~~~~~~~~~~~~~~~~~~~~~~~~~~~~~~~~~~~~~~~

Chapter 8: Location and Infrastructure

8.1 Choosing the Right Location for Your Business

Selecting the optimal location for your business is a critical decision that can significantly impact its success. In this chapter, we explore factors to consider when choosing the right location for your business and strategies for evaluating potential locations effectively.

1. Market Accessibility:

- **Proximity to Target Market:** Consider the proximity of potential locations to your target market. Choose a location that offers easy access to your target customers, whether they are individuals, businesses, or other organizations.

- **Demographic Analysis:** Conduct demographic analysis of the area surrounding potential locations to ensure alignment with your target market. Consider factors such as population density, income levels, age distribution, and lifestyle preferences.

2. Competitive Landscape:

- **Competitor Analysis:** Evaluate the competitive landscape in potential locations to understand the presence and strength of competitors. Assess factors such as market saturation, competitor positioning, and differentiation strategies.

- **Market Share Opportunities:** Identify underserved or niche markets within potential locations where your business can gain a competitive advantage. Look for opportunities to fill gaps in the market or offer unique value propositions.

3. Accessibility and Visibility:

- **Foot Traffic and Accessibility:** Assess the level of foot traffic and accessibility in potential locations, particularly for retail businesses or those reliant on walk-in customers. Choose a location with high visibility and easy access from main roads or transportation hubs.

- **Parking and Transportation:** Consider parking availability and public transportation options for both customers and employees. Ensure that the location provides convenient parking facilities or is easily accessible by public transit.

4. Infrastructure and Amenities:

- **Facility Requirements:** Evaluate the infrastructure and amenities available in potential locations to meet your business needs. Consider factors such as building size, layout, utilities, internet connectivity, and compliance with zoning regulations.

- **Nearby Services:** Assess the availability of essential services and amenities in the vicinity of potential locations, such as restaurants, banks, post offices, healthcare facilities, and recreational areas. Access to these amenities can enhance the convenience and quality of life for employees and customers.

5. Cost Considerations:

- **Real Estate Costs:** Compare real estate costs, including lease or purchase prices, property taxes, and maintenance expenses, across potential locations. Factor in the overall affordability and long-term sustainability of each option.

- **Operating Expenses:** Evaluate other operating expenses associated with each location, such as utilities, insurance, security, and maintenance. Determine the total cost of occupancy for each location to make an informed decision.

6. Regulatory and Legal Factors:
- **Zoning Regulations:** Familiarize yourself with zoning regulations and land use restrictions in potential locations to ensure compliance with local ordinances. Verify that the intended use of the property aligns with zoning requirements and obtain any necessary permits or approvals.

- **Legal Considerations:** Consider any legal implications or contractual obligations associated with leasing or purchasing property in each location. Consult with legal advisors to review lease agreements, negotiate terms, and mitigate risks.

Choosing the right location for your business is a critical strategic decision that requires careful consideration of various factors, including market accessibility, competitive landscape, accessibility and visibility, infrastructure and amenities, cost considerations, and regulatory and legal factors. By conducting thorough research, analyzing potential locations systematically, and weighing the pros and cons of each option, you can make an informed decision that positions your business for success and facilitates its growth and prosperity in the long term. Embrace the opportunity to find the perfect location that aligns with your business goals, enhances your competitiveness, and creates value for your customers and stakeholders.

~~~~~~~~~~~~~~~~~~~
~~~~~~~~~~~~~~~~~~~

8.2 Setting Up Home-based vs. Commercial Office Space

Choosing between a home-based and commercial office space is a significant decision that impacts your business operations, expenses, and overall success. In this chapter, we explore the considerations involved in selecting the appropriate workspace for your business needs.

1. Home-based Office:

- **Cost Savings:** Operating your business from home can significantly reduce overhead costs associated with renting or purchasing commercial office space. You can save on expenses such as rent, utilities, insurance, and commuting.

- **Flexibility:** Home-based businesses offer greater flexibility in terms of work hours, schedule, and lifestyle. You have the freedom to set your own hours, work remotely, and balance professional and personal commitments more effectively.

- **Comfort and Convenience:** Working from home provides a familiar and comfortable environment, with easy access to amenities and facilities. You can enjoy the convenience of being close to family, pets, and personal resources.

2. Commercial Office Space:

- **Professional Image:** Establishing a presence in a commercial office space can enhance your business's credibility and professionalism. A dedicated office space conveys stability, legitimacy, and seriousness to clients, partners, and investors.

- **Collaboration and Networking:** Commercial office spaces offer opportunities for collaboration, networking, and knowledge sharing with other businesses and professionals sharing the same space. You can benefit from shared resources, amenities, and community events.

- **Scalability and Growth:** Renting or leasing commercial office space allows for scalability and growth as your business expands. You can accommodate additional staff, equipment, and resources more easily in a dedicated office environment.

3. Considerations for Home-based Offices:
- **Zoning and Regulations:** Check local zoning regulations and homeowners' association rules to ensure that operating a business from your home is permitted. Obtain any necessary permits or licenses and comply with legal and tax requirements.

- **Workspace Setup:** Create a dedicated workspace within your home that is conducive to productivity and professionalism. Consider factors such as lighting, noise levels, ergonomic furniture, and privacy to optimize your work environment.

- **Technology and Connectivity:** Ensure reliable internet connectivity and invest in necessary technology and equipment to support your home-based operations. Set up a professional communication system, including phone, email, and video conferencing tools.

4. Considerations for Commercial Office Spaces:
- **Location and Accessibility:** Choose a commercial office location that is convenient for employees, clients, and suppliers. Consider factors such as proximity to transportation hubs, parking availability, and amenities in the surrounding area.

- **Lease Terms and Costs:** Evaluate lease terms, rental rates, and additional costs associated with commercial office space, such as utilities, maintenance, and security. Negotiate favorable lease terms and budget carefully to avoid financial strain.

- **Space Planning and Design:** Design your commercial office space to optimize productivity, collaboration, and employee satisfaction. Consider factors such as layout, office configuration, common areas, and amenities to create a functional and inspiring work environment.

Choosing between a home-based and commercial office space involves weighing various factors related to cost, flexibility, professionalism, scalability, and personal preference. Evaluate your business needs, budget constraints, growth plans, and lifestyle considerations carefully to make an informed decision that aligns with your long-term goals and objectives. Whether you opt for a home-based setup or a commercial office space, embrace the opportunity to create a workspace that supports your productivity, fosters creativity, and contributes to the success of your business.

8.3 Assessing Infrastructure Needs and Accessibility

Before establishing your business, it's crucial to assess the infrastructure needs and ensure accessibility to essential resources and services. In this chapter, we explore the considerations involved in evaluating infrastructure requirements and ensuring accessibility for your business.

1. Infrastructure Needs Assessment:

- **Physical Infrastructure:** Evaluate the physical infrastructure required to support your business operations, such as office space, manufacturing facilities, storage facilities, and utilities. Determine the size, layout, and specifications needed for each infrastructure component.

- **Technological Infrastructure:** Assess the technological infrastructure necessary to support your business activities, including computer systems, telecommunications equipment, internet connectivity, and software applications. Ensure that your technology infrastructure is robust, scalable, and secure.

2. Accessibility to Resources:

- **Transportation and Logistics:** Consider the accessibility of transportation networks, including roads, highways, railways, ports, and airports. Evaluate the proximity of potential locations to transportation hubs and logistics facilities to facilitate the movement of goods and materials.

- **Supply Chain:** Assess the availability and reliability of suppliers, vendors, and distributors within your chosen location. Ensure that your supply chain is resilient and capable of meeting your business's needs in terms of quality, quantity, and timeliness.

- **Workforce Availability:** Evaluate the availability of skilled labor and workforce talent in the area surrounding your business location. Consider factors such as population demographics, education levels, training programs, and employment trends to ensure access to a qualified workforce.

3. Accessibility to Services:

- **Utilities and Infrastructure:** Ensure access to essential utilities such as electricity, water, gas, sewage, and telecommunications infrastructure. Evaluate the reliability, capacity, and cost of utility services to support your business operations effectively.

- **Business Support Services:** Assess the availability of business support services such as banking, legal, accounting, insurance, and consulting services. Establish relationships with service providers who can offer expertise and assistance in navigating regulatory requirements and operational challenges.

4. Regulatory Compliance:

- **Zoning and Land Use:** Familiarize yourself with zoning regulations, land use restrictions, and building codes applicable to your chosen location. Ensure compliance with local ordinances and obtain any necessary permits or approvals for your business activities.

- **Environmental Regulations:** Consider environmental regulations and sustainability initiatives that may impact your business operations. Implement environmentally friendly practices and compliance measures to minimize your ecological footprint and mitigate regulatory risks.

5. Accessibility for Customers and Stakeholders:

- **Customer Convenience:** Consider the convenience and accessibility of your business location for customers, clients, and stakeholders. Choose a location that is easily accessible by public transportation, has ample parking facilities, and is located in a safe and desirable neighborhood.

- **Community Engagement:** Engage with the local community and build relationships with neighboring businesses, residents, and civic organizations. Participate in community events, sponsorships, and initiatives to contribute positively to the community and enhance your brand reputation.

Assessing infrastructure needs and ensuring accessibility to essential resources and services are critical steps in setting up your business for success. By evaluating physical and technological infrastructure requirements, assessing accessibility to resources and services, ensuring regulatory compliance, and prioritizing accessibility for customers and stakeholders, you can establish a strong foundation for your business operations. Embrace the opportunity to create a conducive environment that supports growth, innovation, and sustainability, positioning your business for long-term success and prosperity.

~~~~~~~~~~~~~~~~~
~~~~~~~~~~~~~~~~~

9.1 Hiring Your First Employees or Outsourcing

As your business grows, the decision to hire your first employees or outsource certain functions becomes crucial. In this chapter, we delve into the considerations involved in hiring employees versus outsourcing and provide guidance on making the right choice for your business.

1. Hiring Employees:

- **Identifying Staffing Needs:** Assess your business's staffing needs based on current workload, projected growth, and operational requirements. Determine the roles and skill sets needed to support your business objectives.

- **Recruitment and Selection:** Develop a recruitment strategy to attract qualified candidates for your job openings. Utilize job boards, professional networks, referrals, and recruitment agencies to source candidates. Conduct thorough interviews and assessments to evaluate candidates' qualifications, experience, and cultural fit.

- **Employment Contracts:** Draft employment contracts outlining terms and conditions of employment, including job responsibilities, compensation, benefits, and employment status (full-time, part-time, or contract). Ensure compliance with labor laws and regulations governing employment relationships.

2. Outsourcing:

- **Identifying Outsourcing Opportunities:** Evaluate tasks and functions within your business that can be outsourced to third-party providers. Consider outsourcing non-core activities such as accounting, payroll, IT support, customer service, and marketing to specialized service providers.

- **Vendor Selection:** Research and vet potential outsourcing vendors to ensure they have the expertise, resources, and track record to meet your business needs. Request proposals, conduct interviews, and assess vendor capabilities before making a decision.

- **Service Level Agreements (SLAs):** Establish clear service level agreements (SLAs) with outsourcing vendors outlining expectations, deliverables, performance metrics, and remedies for non-compliance. Ensure that SLAs align with your business objectives and provide accountability and transparency.

3. Considerations for Hiring Employees:

- **Costs and Liabilities:** Evaluate the costs and liabilities associated with hiring employees, including salaries, benefits, payroll taxes, workers' compensation insurance, and legal compliance. Consider the long-term financial implications and budget accordingly.

- **Training and Development:** Invest in training and development programs to onboard and develop your employees effectively. Provide ongoing support, feedback, and opportunities for growth and advancement to enhance employee engagement and retention.

- **Culture and Team Dynamics:** Foster a positive work culture and team dynamics to promote collaboration, communication, and morale among your employees. Lead by example and cultivate a supportive and inclusive workplace environment.

4. Considerations for Outsourcing:

- **Cost Effectiveness:** Assess the cost-effectiveness of outsourcing compared to hiring employees for specific functions. Consider factors such as upfront costs, ongoing expenses, scalability, and flexibility when evaluating outsourcing options.

- **Quality and Reliability:** Ensure that outsourcing vendors have a proven track record of delivering high-quality services reliably and consistently. Review client testimonials, case studies, and references to gauge vendor performance and reliability.

- **Communication and Collaboration:** Maintain open communication and collaboration with outsourcing vendors to ensure alignment with your business goals and priorities. Establish regular check-ins, reporting mechanisms, and escalation procedures to address issues and drive accountability.

5. Decision-making Process:

- **Assessing Needs and Objectives:** Evaluate your business needs, objectives, and constraints to determine whether hiring employees or outsourcing is the best solution. Consider factors such as expertise required, cost considerations, scalability, flexibility, and strategic alignment.

- **Risk Assessment:** Assess the risks associated with each option, including financial risks, operational risks, legal risks, and reputational risks. Mitigate risks through careful planning, due diligence, and risk management strategies.

- **Making an Informed Decision:** Make an informed decision based on a comprehensive analysis of the pros and cons of hiring employees versus outsourcing. Consider the short-term and long-term implications for your business and choose the option that best aligns with your goals and objectives.

Deciding whether to hire employees or outsource certain functions is a pivotal decision that impacts your business's growth, efficiency, and success. By carefully assessing your business needs, evaluating the advantages and disadvantages of each option, and considering factors such as cost, expertise, scalability, and strategic alignment, you can make an informed decision that positions your business for success. Embrace the opportunity to build a talented team or leverage external expertise to drive innovation, productivity, and competitiveness in your industry.

~~~~~~~~~~~~~~~~~~~~~~~~~~~~~~~~~~~~~~
~~~~~~~~~~~~~~~~~~~~~~~~~~~~~~~~~~~~~~

9.2 Creating HR Policies and Employee Handbook

Establishing comprehensive HR policies and an employee handbook is essential for setting clear expectations, promoting consistency, and ensuring compliance within your organization. In this chapter, we delve into the process of creating HR policies and developing an employee handbook tailored to your business needs.

1. Policy Development Process:

- **Identify Key Areas:** Determine the key areas that require HR policies within your organization, such as recruitment, hiring, onboarding, compensation, benefits, performance management, leave management, code of conduct, and disciplinary procedures.

- **Legal Compliance:** Ensure that HR policies comply with applicable labor laws, regulations, and industry standards. Consult with legal experts or HR professionals to review and validate policies for legal compliance and adherence to best practices.

- **Customization:** Customize HR policies to reflect the unique culture, values, and operational requirements of your organization. Consider factors such as company size, industry, geographical location, and workforce demographics when developing policies.

2. Components of HR Policies:

- **Policy Statements:** Clearly articulate policy statements that outline the organization's stance, expectations, and guidelines regarding specific HR topics. Use concise language and avoid ambiguity to facilitate understanding and compliance.

- **Scope and Applicability:** Define the scope and applicability of each policy, including who is covered by the policy, under what circumstances it applies, and any exceptions or special considerations.

- **Procedures and Processes:** Detail the procedures and processes for implementing, enforcing, and administering each policy. Provide step-by-step instructions, forms, templates, and resources to facilitate compliance and consistency.

3. Employee Handbook Development:

- **Introduction and Welcome Message:** Start the employee handbook with an introduction and welcome message from senior leadership, emphasizing the organization's mission, values, and commitment to employees.

- **Table of Contents:** Provide a comprehensive table of contents outlining the structure and contents of the employee handbook for easy navigation and reference.

- **HR Policies and Procedures:** Include detailed HR policies and procedures covering various aspects of the employee lifecycle, from recruitment and onboarding to performance management and separation.

- **Legal Disclaimers and Acknowledgments:** Include legal disclaimers, confidentiality agreements, and acknowledgments requiring employees to read, understand, and comply with the policies outlined in the handbook.

- **Communication and Updates:** Establish a process for communicating updates, revisions, and amendments to the employee handbook. Encourage feedback from employees and stakeholders to ensure continuous improvement and relevance.

4. Accessibility and Distribution:

- **Accessibility:** Ensure that the employee handbook is accessible to all employees, whether in print or electronic format. Provide access to the handbook through the company intranet, employee portal, or other centralized platforms.

- **Distribution:** Distribute copies of the employee handbook to all employees upon hire and whenever updates or revisions are made. Require employees to sign an acknowledgment form confirming receipt and understanding of the handbook.

5. Training and Compliance:

- **Training Programs:** Conduct training sessions or orientation programs to familiarize employees with the contents of the employee handbook. Provide opportunities for interactive discussion, clarification, and Q&A sessions to ensure comprehension and buy-in.

- **Compliance Monitoring:** Monitor compliance with HR policies outlined in the employee handbook through regular audits, assessments, and feedback mechanisms. Address any violations or discrepancies promptly and consistently.

Creating HR policies and an employee handbook is a critical step in establishing a structured and compliant HR framework within your organization. By following a systematic process for policy development, customizing policies to align with your organizational culture and requirements, and ensuring accessibility, distribution, training, and compliance monitoring, you can create an effective and comprehensive resource that guides employee behavior, promotes consistency, and mitigates risks. Embrace the opportunity to communicate expectations clearly, foster a positive work environment, and build trust and accountability among your workforce through well-defined HR policies and procedures.

~~~~~~
~~~~~~

9.3 Managing Employee Performance and Engagement

Effective management of employee performance and engagement is essential for maximizing productivity, fostering a positive work culture, and achieving business objectives. In this chapter, we explore strategies and best practices for managing employee performance and promoting engagement within your organization.

1. Performance Management Process:

- **Goal Setting:** Establish clear, measurable, and achievable goals for each employee aligned with organizational objectives. Ensure that goals are specific, relevant, time-bound, and periodically reviewed and adjusted as needed.

- **Regular Feedback:** Provide ongoing feedback and coaching to employees to support their development and performance improvement. Conduct regular check-ins, performance reviews, and one-on-one meetings to discuss progress, challenges, and opportunities for growth.

- **Performance Appraisals:** Conduct formal performance appraisals or evaluations at regular intervals to assess employee performance against predetermined goals and expectations. Use objective criteria, performance metrics, and qualitative assessments to provide a comprehensive evaluation.

- **Recognition and Rewards:** Recognize and reward employees for their contributions, achievements, and outstanding performance. Implement formal recognition programs, incentives, bonuses, and awards to motivate and retain top performers.

2. Employee Engagement Strategies:
- **Open Communication:** Foster open, transparent, and two-way communication channels between management and employees. Encourage feedback, suggestions, and ideas from employees and provide avenues for them to voice concerns or grievances.

- **Professional Development:** Invest in employee training, development, and career growth opportunities to enhance skills, knowledge, and capabilities. Offer workshops, seminars, certifications, and mentorship programs to support continuous learning and career advancement.

- **Work-Life Balance:** Promote work-life balance initiatives and flexible work arrangements to accommodate employees' personal and professional needs. Provide options such as telecommuting, flexible scheduling, and paid time off to help employees manage their work commitments and personal responsibilities.

- **Employee Wellness:** Prioritize employee health and well-being by offering wellness programs, health benefits, and resources to support physical, mental, and emotional wellness. Create a supportive and inclusive work environment that values diversity, equity, and inclusion.

3. Performance Improvement Plans (PIPs):

- **Identifying Performance Issues:** Identify performance issues or areas of improvement through ongoing feedback, performance evaluations, and observation. Address performance issues promptly and constructively to prevent them from escalating.

- **Creating Actionable Plans:** Develop performance improvement plans (PIPs) outlining specific goals, expectations, timelines, and support mechanisms for employees to address performance deficiencies. Collaborate with employees to create actionable plans tailored to their needs and circumstances.

- **Monitoring and Support:** Monitor progress and provide ongoing support, guidance, and resources to employees undergoing performance improvement plans. Offer coaching, training, and mentoring to help employees develop the skills and competencies needed to succeed.

4. Employee Engagement Surveys:

- **Conducting Surveys:** Conduct regular employee engagement surveys to assess overall satisfaction, morale, and engagement levels within the organization. Use survey data to identify trends, areas of improvement, and opportunities for enhancing employee experience.

- **Analyzing Feedback:** Analyze survey results and feedback to identify key drivers of engagement, areas of concern, and actionable insights for organizational improvement. Prioritize initiatives based on survey findings and involve employees in decision-making and problem-solving processes.

- **Action Planning:** Develop action plans to address identified areas of improvement and implement initiatives to enhance employee engagement and satisfaction. Communicate survey results, action plans, and progress updates transparently to employees to demonstrate commitment to their well-being and feedback.

Managing employee performance and engagement is a continuous process that requires proactive communication, feedback, support, and collaboration between management and employees. By implementing effective performance management processes, engaging employees through open communication, recognition, and development opportunities, addressing performance issues promptly and constructively, and leveraging employee feedback to drive organizational improvement, you can create a positive work environment where employees feel valued, motivated, and empowered to contribute to the organization's success. Embrace the opportunity to cultivate a culture of high performance, accountability, and engagement that drives business growth and fosters employee satisfaction and retention.

~~~~~~~~~~~~~~~~~~~~~~~~~~~~~~~~~~~~~
~~~~~~~~~~~~~~~~~~~~~~~~~~~~~~~~~~~~~

10.1 Streamlining Business Processes and Workflow

Efficient business processes and workflow are essential for optimizing productivity, minimizing waste, and delivering value to customers. In this chapter, we explore strategies for streamlining business processes and workflow to enhance operational efficiency and effectiveness.

1. Process Mapping and Analysis:

- **Identify Core Processes:** Identify the core processes and workflows that drive value creation and contribute to your business's success. Map out each process step-by-step to understand the flow of activities, inputs, outputs, and dependencies.

- **Analyze Process Efficiency:** Analyze each process to identify inefficiencies, bottlenecks, redundancies, and areas for improvement. Look for opportunities to streamline workflows, eliminate waste, and improve cycle times to enhance overall efficiency.

- **Root Cause Analysis:** Conduct root cause analysis to identify underlying issues and factors contributing to process inefficiencies. Use techniques such as fishbone diagrams, Pareto analysis, and 5 Whys to identify root causes and prioritize improvement initiatives.

2. Automation and Technology Integration:

- **Identify Automation Opportunities:** Identify opportunities to automate repetitive tasks, manual processes, and low-value activities using technology solutions such as workflow automation software, robotic process automation (RPA), and artificial intelligence (AI).

- **Select Appropriate Tools:** Select and implement technology tools and systems that align with your business needs, budget, and objectives. Evaluate options such as CRM systems, ERP systems, project management software, and collaboration tools to streamline operations and improve workflow.

- **Integration and Connectivity:** Ensure seamless integration and connectivity between different systems, applications, and platforms to facilitate data exchange, information flow, and process synchronization. Implement APIs, middleware, and integration platforms to connect disparate systems and enable real-time data sharing.

3. Standardization and Documentation:

- **Develop Standard Operating Procedures (SOPs):** Develop clear, comprehensive standard operating procedures (SOPs) for each business process and workflow. Document step-by-step instructions, best practices, and guidelines to ensure consistency, compliance, and quality.

- **Training and Implementation:** Train employees on SOPs and ensure consistent implementation across the organization. Provide resources, training materials, and job aids to support employees in following SOPs effectively and consistently.

- **Continuous Improvement:** Establish a culture of continuous improvement by regularly reviewing and updating SOPs based on feedback, lessons learned, and evolving business needs. Encourage employee involvement in process improvement initiatives and recognize contributions to driving efficiency and effectiveness.

4. Performance Monitoring and Optimization:
- **Establish Key Performance Indicators (KPIs):** Define and track key performance indicators (KPIs) to measure process performance, identify trends, and monitor progress towards goals. Use KPIs such as cycle time, throughput, error rates, and customer satisfaction to assess process effectiveness.

- **Root Cause Analysis:** Conduct root cause analysis to identify underlying issues and factors contributing to process deviations, inefficiencies, or failures. Take corrective actions to address root causes and prevent recurrence of problems.

- **Continuous Monitoring and Optimization:** Implement systems and processes for continuous monitoring, measurement, and optimization of business processes and workflows. Use techniques such as Lean Six Sigma, Total Quality Management (TQM), and Kaizen to drive ongoing improvement and innovation.

Optimize business processes to boost efficiency, cut waste, and deliver value. Map, analyze, and automate tasks, standardize procedures, and monitor performance for ongoing improvement. Streamlining operations empowers employees and delights customers with efficient workflows.

10.2 Managing Inventory and Supply Chain Logistics

Effective inventory management and supply chain logistics are essential for ensuring product availability, minimizing costs, and delivering superior customer service. In this chapter, we explore strategies and best practices for managing inventory and optimizing supply chain logistics.

1. Inventory Management:

- **Demand Forecasting:** Utilize historical sales data, market trends, and customer feedback to forecast demand accurately. Develop demand forecasts for each product SKU to optimize inventory levels and prevent stockouts or overstock situations.

- **Inventory Classification:** Classify inventory items based on factors such as demand variability, value, and criticality. Use techniques like ABC analysis to prioritize inventory management efforts and allocate resources effectively.

- **Safety Stock Management:** Maintain safety stock levels to buffer against demand variability, supply chain disruptions, and lead time uncertainties. Determine safety stock quantities based on factors such as service level targets, lead times, and demand variability.

2. Supply Chain Logistics:

- **Supplier Management:** Build strong supplier relationships for reliability, quality, and cost-effectiveness. Negotiate favorable terms for timely deliveries, competitive pricing, and flexible payment.

- **Inventory Replenishment:** Implement inventory replenishment strategies such as just-in-time (JIT), economic order quantity (EOQ), and vendor-managed inventory (VMI) to optimize inventory levels and minimize carrying costs. Automate replenishment processes where possible to improve efficiency and accuracy.

- **Transportation and Distribution:** Optimize transportation and distribution networks to minimize lead times, transportation costs, and carbon footprint. Utilize transportation management systems (TMS) and route optimization software to optimize delivery routes, consolidate shipments, and reduce empty miles.

3. Warehouse Management:

- **Warehouse Layout and Design:** Design warehouse layouts that maximize space utilization, efficiency, and accessibility. Implement storage systems, shelving, and racking solutions to organize inventory and facilitate picking, packing, and shipping operations.

- **Inventory Tracking and Visibility:** Implement inventory tracking systems such as barcoding, RFID, and warehouse management systems (WMS) to track inventory movements, locations, and quantities in real-time. Enhance visibility into inventory levels, stock movements, and order status to improve accuracy and responsiveness.

- **Order Fulfillment:** Streamline order fulfillment processes to reduce cycle times, improve accuracy, and enhance customer satisfaction. Implement picking, packing, and shipping workflows that prioritize efficiency, accuracy, and timeliness.

4. Risk Management and Contingency Planning:

- **Risk Assessment:** Identify potential risks and vulnerabilities within the supply chain, including supplier reliability, geopolitical factors, natural disasters, and economic uncertainties. Conduct risk assessments and scenario planning to evaluate the impact of potential disruptions and develop mitigation strategies.

- **Supplier Diversification:** Diversify your supplier base to reduce dependency on a single source and mitigate supply chain risks. Develop alternative sourcing strategies, qualify backup suppliers, and maintain relationships with multiple vendors to ensure continuity of supply.

- **Contingency Planning:** Develop contingency plans and business continuity strategies to address supply chain disruptions and emergencies. Establish protocols for communication, decision-making, and response coordination to minimize downtime and mitigate financial and reputational impacts.

Managing inventory and supply chain logistics effectively is crucial for operational efficiency, cost minimization, and customer satisfaction. Implementing best practices in management, logistics, and risk mitigation creates a resilient supply chain, driving business growth. Streamline operations and optimize your supply chain to gain a competitive advantage.

~~~~~~
~~~~~~

10.3 Quality Control and Customer Service Standards

Maintaining high-quality products and services while providing exceptional customer service is paramount to the success and sustainability of any business. In this chapter, we delve into the importance of quality control and customer service standards and strategies for ensuring customer satisfaction and loyalty.

1. Quality Control Processes:

- **Quality Assurance:** Implement quality assurance processes to ensure that products and services meet or exceed customer expectations and industry standards. Develop quality control checklists, procedures, and standards to monitor and evaluate product/service quality throughout the production/service delivery process.

- **Quality Inspections:** Conduct regular inspections and audits to identify defects, deviations, or non-conformities in products, services, or processes. Utilize statistical quality control techniques, sampling methods, and inspection tools to assess quality and detect abnormalities.

- **Continuous Improvement:** Foster a culture of continuous improvement by soliciting feedback from customers, employees, and stakeholders. Use quality metrics, performance indicators, and benchmarking to identify areas for improvement and implement corrective actions.

2. Customer Service Standards:

- **Customer-Centric Culture:** Cultivate a customer-centric culture within your organization that prioritizes customer satisfaction and loyalty. Empower employees to go above and beyond to meet customer needs, resolve issues, and exceed expectations.

- **Clear Communication:** Establish clear communication channels and protocols for interacting with customers and addressing their inquiries, concerns, and feedback. Provide multiple touchpoints for customer support, including phone, email, chat, and social media, to ensure accessibility and responsiveness.

- **Service Level Agreements (SLAs):** Define service level agreements (SLAs) outlining response times, resolution times, and service guarantees for customer inquiries and support requests. Monitor SLA adherence and performance metrics to track service quality and identify areas for improvement.

3. Training and Development:

- **Employee Training:** Provide comprehensive training and development programs to equip employees with the knowledge, skills, and tools needed to deliver exceptional customer service. Offer training on product knowledge, communication skills, conflict resolution, and service excellence.

- **Role-Playing and Simulation:** Conduct role-playing exercises and simulations to simulate real-world customer interactions and scenarios. Practice handling challenging situations, addressing customer complaints, and delivering effective solutions in a controlled environment.

- **Continuous Feedback and Coaching:** Provide ongoing feedback, coaching, and performance evaluations to support employees in improving their customer service skills and competencies. Recognize and reward employees for demonstrating outstanding service and exceeding performance expectations.

4. Customer Feedback and Satisfaction:
- **Feedback Mechanisms:** Implement feedback mechanisms such as surveys, reviews, and feedback forms to gather input from customers about their experiences with your products and services. Use feedback to identify areas for improvement, address customer concerns, and enhance service quality.

- **Customer Satisfaction Metrics:** Measure customer satisfaction using metrics such as Net Promoter Score (NPS), customer satisfaction score (CSAT), and customer effort score (CES). Analyze survey results and customer feedback to identify trends, patterns, and areas of strength and weakness.

- **Continuous Improvement:** Use customer feedback and satisfaction data to drive continuous improvement initiatives and service enhancements. Take proactive steps to address customer pain points, streamline processes, and deliver value-added services that delight customers and foster loyalty.

Quality control and customer service standards are integral components of successful operations and supply chain management. By prioritizing quality, implementing robust quality control processes, setting high customer service standards, and continuously striving for improvement, you can build a reputation for excellence, earn customer trust and loyalty, and drive business growth and success. Embrace the opportunity to exceed customer expectations, differentiate your brand, and create memorable experiences that keep customers coming back for more.

~~~~~~~~~~~~~~~~~~~~~~~
~~~~~~~~~~~~~~~~~~~~~~~

11.1 Leveraging Technology for Business Efficiency

In today's digital age, leveraging technology is essential for small businesses to streamline operations, enhance productivity, and stay competitive. This chapter explores the myriad of technology tools available to small businesses and how they can be utilized to improve efficiency across various aspects of business operations.

1. Cloud-Based Solutions:

- **Data Storage and Collaboration:** Utilize cloud-based storage solutions such as Google Drive, Dropbox, or OneDrive for storing and sharing documents, files, and data securely. Enable real-time collaboration and document editing to facilitate teamwork and enhance productivity.

- **Project Management:** Implement cloud-based project management tools like Asana, Trello, or Basecamp to organize tasks, track progress, and manage workflows effectively. Assign responsibilities, set deadlines, and communicate project updates seamlessly within a centralized platform.

2. Communication Tools:

- **Email and Messaging Platforms:** Use email services like Gmail or Outlook and instant messaging platforms such as Slack or Microsoft Teams for internal and external communication. Streamline communication, share information, and collaborate with team members and clients in real-time.

- **Video Conferencing:** Conduct virtual meetings, client consultations, and team brainstorming sessions using video conferencing tools like Zoom, Skype, or Google Meet. Enhance remote collaboration, minimize travel costs, and maintain face-to-face communication regardless of geographical distances.

3. Customer Relationship Management (CRM) Systems:

- **Client Data Management:** Implement a CRM system such as HubSpot, Salesforce, or Zoho CRM to centralize customer data, track interactions, and manage relationships effectively. Streamline lead management, automate follow-up tasks, and personalize communication to enhance customer satisfaction and loyalty.

- **Sales Pipeline Management:** Use CRM tools to visualize and manage your sales pipeline, track opportunities, and forecast revenue. Monitor sales activities, analyze performance metrics, and identify areas for improvement to drive sales growth and maximize revenue.

4. Accounting and Financial Management:

- **Bookkeeping Software:** Invest in accounting software like QuickBooks, Xero, or FreshBooks to manage your business finances efficiently. Automate bookkeeping tasks, track expenses, generate invoices, and reconcile bank transactions seamlessly within a user-friendly interface.

- **Expense Management:** Utilize expense tracking apps or platforms such as Expensify or Receipt Bank to capture receipts, categorize expenses, and streamline reimbursement processes. Simplify expense reporting, ensure compliance, and gain insights into spending patterns to optimize budgets and control costs.

5. Marketing Automation Tools:

- **Email Marketing:** Leverage email marketing platforms like Mailchimp, Constant Contact, or ConvertKit to automate email campaigns, nurture leads, and engage with customers effectively. Create personalized email sequences, segment your audience, and track campaign performance to drive engagement and conversions.

- **Social Media Management:** Use social media management tools such as Hootsuite, Buffer, or Sprout Social to schedule posts, monitor mentions, and analyze social media performance across multiple platforms. Streamline content creation, manage social interactions, and measure the impact of your social media efforts.

6. Website and E-commerce Platforms:

- **Website Builder:** Build a professional-looking website using website builder platforms like WordPress, Wix, or Squarespace. Customize templates, add content, and optimize for search engines to create a compelling online presence that attracts and engages visitors.

- **E-commerce Integration:** Integrate e-commerce platforms such as Shopify, WooCommerce, or BigCommerce with your website to sell products or services online. Manage inventory, process orders, and accept payments securely to expand your reach and increase sales opportunities.

Leveraging technology is crucial for small businesses to enhance efficiency, productivity, and competitiveness in today's fast-paced digital landscape. By embracing cloud-based solutions, communication tools, CRM systems, accounting software, marketing automation tools, and website/e-commerce platforms, small businesses can streamline operations, automate repetitive tasks, and focus on driving growth and innovation. Embrace the power of technology to transform your business operations, delight your customers, and achieve long-term success and sustainability.

~~~~~~
~~~~~~

11.2 Essential Software and Tools for Small Businesses

In the digital age, small businesses have access to a plethora of software and tools that can streamline operations, improve efficiency, and drive growth. This chapter explores essential software and tools that every small business should consider incorporating into their operations.

1. Accounting Software:

- **QuickBooks:** A widely used accounting software that simplifies bookkeeping, invoicing, expense tracking, and financial reporting for small businesses.

- **Xero:** Another popular accounting solution that offers features such as bank reconciliation, payroll processing, and customizable financial reports.

2. Project Management Tools:

- **Asana:** A versatile project management tool that helps teams organize tasks, track progress, and collaborate effectively on projects of all sizes.

- **Trello:** A visual project management tool that uses boards, lists, and cards to streamline task management and project workflows.

3. Customer Relationship Management (CRM) Systems:

- **HubSpot CRM:** A free CRM platform that enables small businesses to manage contacts, track deals, and automate sales processes to nurture leads and grow relationships.

- **Salesforce Essentials:** A CRM solution designed specifically for small businesses, offering features such as contact management, lead scoring, and email integration.

4. Communication and Collaboration Tools:

- **Slack:** A popular messaging platform that facilitates real-time communication and collaboration among team members through channels, direct messages, and file sharing.

- **Microsoft Teams:** An integrated collaboration platform that combines chat, video conferencing, file storage, and app integration within the Microsoft 365 ecosystem.

5. Email Marketing Software:

- **Mailchimp:** An easy-to-use email marketing platform that allows small businesses to create and send email campaigns, automate marketing workflows, and analyze campaign performance.

- **Constant Contact:** A comprehensive email marketing tool that offers customizable templates, list management, and marketing automation features to engage subscribers and drive conversions.

6. Website Builders:

- **WordPress:** A versatile content management system (CMS) that enables small businesses to build and customize professional websites using customizable themes and plugins.

- **Wix:** An intuitive website builder that offers drag-and-drop functionality, pre-designed templates, and built-in SEO tools to create visually stunning websites with ease.

7. Social Media Management Platforms:

- **Hootsuite:** A social media management tool that allows small businesses to schedule posts, monitor mentions, and analyze social media performance across multiple platforms from a single dashboard.

- **Buffer:** An all-in-one social media solution that simplifies content publishing, engagement, and analytics for small businesses looking to grow their social presence.

These essential software and tools serve as indispensable assets for small businesses seeking to streamline operations, improve productivity, and enhance customer engagement. By leveraging accounting software, project management tools, CRM systems, communication platforms, email marketing software, website builders, and social media management platforms, small businesses can optimize their workflows, automate routine tasks, and focus on driving growth and success in today's competitive marketplace. Embrace the power of technology to propel your small business forward and achieve your goals with confidence.

11.3 Data Security and Privacy Considerations

In an increasingly digital world, safeguarding sensitive data and maintaining customer privacy is paramount for small businesses. This chapter explores essential considerations and best practices for ensuring data security and protecting customer privacy in the digital age.

1. Secure Data Storage:
- **Cloud-Based Solutions:** Consider using reputable cloud storage providers such as Google Cloud Platform, Microsoft Azure, or Amazon Web Services (AWS) to store sensitive business data securely. Implement encryption and access controls to protect data from unauthorized access or breaches.

2. Data Backup and Recovery:
- **Regular Backups:** Establish a regular schedule for backing up critical business data to prevent data loss in the event of hardware failures, cyberattacks, or natural disasters. Utilize backup solutions such as cloud backup services or on-premises backup systems to ensure data redundancy and resilience.

3. Strong Authentication Measures:
- **Multi-Factor Authentication (MFA):** Implement multi-factor authentication for accessing sensitive systems, applications, and data. Require users to verify their identity through multiple factors such as passwords, biometrics, or one-time codes to mitigate the risk of unauthorized access.

4. Employee Training and Awareness:

- **Security Awareness Training:** Provide comprehensive security awareness training to employees to educate them about common cyber threats, phishing attacks, and best practices for safeguarding sensitive information. Empower employees to recognize and report suspicious activities or security incidents promptly.

5. Compliance with Data Protection Regulations:

- **GDPR Compliance:** Ensure compliance with the General Data Protection Regulation (GDPR) if your business operates in the European Union (EU) or handles personal data of EU residents. Implement measures such as data encryption, consent management, and data subject rights fulfillment to adhere to GDPR requirements.

- **HIPAA Compliance:** If your business deals with healthcare information, adhere to the Health Insurance Portability and Accountability Act (HIPAA) regulations to protect the privacy and security of patient data. Implement safeguards such as access controls, encryption, and audit trails to maintain HIPAA compliance.

6. Incident Response Plan:

- **Develop a Response Plan:** Develop an incident response plan outlining steps to take in the event of a data breach, cyberattack, or security incident. Define roles and responsibilities, establish communication protocols, and outline procedures for containing, mitigating, and reporting security breaches.

7. Regular Security Audits and Assessments:
- **Security Audits:** Conduct regular security audits and assessments to evaluate the effectiveness of your cybersecurity measures, identify vulnerabilities, and address gaps in security controls. Engage third-party cybersecurity firms or consultants to perform comprehensive security assessments and penetration testing.

Data security and privacy are critical considerations for small businesses operating in the digital landscape. By implementing robust security measures, providing employee training, ensuring compliance with data protection regulations, and developing incident response plans, small businesses can mitigate the risks of data breaches, protect customer privacy, and maintain trust and credibility with their stakeholders. Prioritize data security and privacy considerations to safeguard your business assets and reputation in today's interconnected world.

Part IV: Growing Your Business

Chapter 12: Scaling and Expansion Strategies

12.1 Identifying Growth Opportunities and Market Expansion

Expanding your business requires careful planning and strategic decision-making to capitalize on growth opportunities and penetrate new markets. In this chapter, we explore effective strategies for identifying growth opportunities and expanding your market reach.

1. Market Research and Analysis:
- **Market Segmentation:** Conduct thorough market research to identify niche markets, segments, or customer demographics that align with your products or services. Analyze market trends, consumer behavior, and competitive landscape to uncover untapped opportunities for growth.

- **SWOT Analysis:** Perform a SWOT analysis (Strengths, Weaknesses, Opportunities, Threats) to assess your business's internal strengths and weaknesses, as well as external opportunities and threats in the market. Use insights from the analysis to inform your growth strategy and mitigate potential risks.

2. Product or Service Innovation:
- **Customer Feedback:** Solicit feedback from existing customers to understand their needs, preferences, and pain points. Use customer insights to innovate and improve your products or services, develop new features, or introduce value-added offerings that differentiate your business in the market.

- **Continuous Improvement:** Embrace a culture of continuous improvement and innovation within your organization. Encourage creativity, experimentation, and collaboration among employees to generate innovative ideas and solutions that drive business growth and customer satisfaction.

3. Geographic Expansion:

- **Market Assessment:** Evaluate potential new markets or geographic regions for expansion based on factors such as population demographics, economic indicators, and competitive landscape. Conduct feasibility studies and market assessments to assess market demand, competition, and regulatory requirements.

- **Entry Strategies:** Determine the most suitable entry strategies for expanding into new markets, such as organic growth, partnerships, franchising, or acquisitions. Develop market entry plans and allocate resources strategically to maximize market penetration and minimize risks.

4. Diversification and Product Extensions:

- **Product Portfolio Analysis:** Assess your existing product or service portfolio to identify opportunities for diversification or product extensions. Explore complementary or related product categories, market segments, or customer needs that align with your core competencies and brand positioning.

- **Risk Management:** Manage risks associated with diversification by conducting thorough market research, feasibility studies, and financial analysis. Mitigate risks through phased rollouts, pilot programs, or partnerships to test new products or markets before committing significant resources.

5. Strategic Partnerships and Alliances:

- **Strategic Networking:** Build strategic partnerships and alliances with other businesses, industry associations, or complementary service providers to leverage synergies and accelerate growth. Collaborate on joint marketing initiatives, co-branding opportunities, or cross-promotional campaigns to reach new audiences and expand your market reach.

- **Distribution Channels:** Explore partnership opportunities with distributors, retailers, or online marketplaces to extend your distribution reach and access new customer segments. Negotiate mutually beneficial agreements and partnerships that enhance your market presence and increase sales channels.

6. Digital Marketing and Online Presence:

- **Digital Marketing Strategies:** Implement digital marketing strategies such as search engine optimization (SEO), content marketing, social media advertising, and email marketing to increase brand visibility, generate leads, and drive website traffic. Target specific audience segments and tailor your messaging to resonate with their needs and preferences.

- **E-commerce Expansion:** Expand your online presence by launching an e-commerce platform or selling through third-party online marketplaces. Optimize your e-commerce website for user experience, mobile responsiveness, and secure transactions to facilitate seamless online shopping experiences for customers.

Identifying growth opportunities and expanding your market reach is essential for scaling your business and achieving long-term success. By conducting market research, innovating products or services, exploring geographic expansion, diversifying your offerings, forming strategic partnerships, and leveraging digital marketing and online channels, you can unlock new avenues for growth and position your business for sustained profitability and competitiveness in the marketplace. Embrace a strategic approach to scaling and expansion, adapt to changing market dynamics, and capitalize on emerging opportunities to drive business growth and achieve your goals.

~~~~~~~~~~~~~~~~~~~~~~~~~
~~~~~~~~~~~~~~~~~~~~~~~~~

12.2 Strategic Partnerships and Collaboration

Strategic partnerships and collaboration are powerful vehicles for accelerating growth, accessing new markets, and leveraging complementary strengths. In this chapter, we explore the importance of strategic partnerships and provide insights into how businesses can forge successful collaborations to drive expansion.

1. Identifying Strategic Partners:

- **Complementary Businesses:** Identify businesses that offer complementary products, services, or expertise that align with your own offerings. Look for synergies and opportunities to create value through collaboration, such as bundling products/services or cross-promotional campaigns.

- **Industry Associations:** Engage with industry associations, trade organizations, or business networks to connect with potential partners and explore collaboration opportunities within your industry or sector.

2. Benefits of Strategic Partnerships:

- **Access to New Markets:** Partnering with established businesses or industry players can provide access to new markets, customer segments, or distribution channels that may be difficult to reach independently.

- **Shared Resources and Expertise:** Collaborating with partners allows businesses to leverage shared resources, capabilities, and expertise to achieve common goals more efficiently and cost-effectively.

- **Risk Mitigation:** Strategic partnerships can help mitigate risks associated with market entry, product development, or expansion by sharing costs, responsibilities, and liabilities with partners.

3. Types of Strategic Partnerships:

- **Distribution Partnerships:** Form partnerships with distributors, retailers, or online marketplaces to extend your product reach and access new customer segments.

- **Technology Partnerships:** Collaborate with technology providers or software vendors to integrate complementary solutions, enhance product functionality, or develop new offerings.

- **Marketing Partnerships:** Partner with influencers, content creators, or other brands to co-create marketing campaigns, sponsor events, or reach new audiences through joint promotional efforts.

4. Key Considerations for Successful Partnerships:

- **Aligned Goals and Values:** Ensure alignment between your business objectives, values, and those of your potential partners to establish a solid foundation for collaboration.

- **Clear Communication and Expectations:** Establish clear communication channels and set expectations upfront regarding roles, responsibilities, and mutual benefits of the partnership.

- **Legal Agreements:** Formalize partnerships with written agreements or contracts that outline terms and conditions, intellectual property rights, and dispute resolution mechanisms to protect both parties' interests.

5. Managing and Nurturing Partnerships:

- **Regular Communication:** Maintain open lines of communication with partners and foster a collaborative relationship through regular meetings, updates, and feedback sessions.

- **Performance Evaluation:** Monitor partnership performance against predefined metrics and KPIs to track progress, identify areas for improvement, and ensure alignment with business objectives.

- **Adaptability and Flexibility:** Be flexible and adaptable in your approach to partnership management and be willing to adjust strategies or tactics as needed to address changing market dynamics or partner needs.

6. Case Studies and Success Stories:

- **Highlight successful partnership examples or case studies from your industry or sector to illustrate the benefits and potential outcomes of strategic collaborations.

- **Share real-world experiences, insights, and lessons learned from businesses that have effectively leveraged partnerships to drive growth, innovation, or market expansion.

Strategic partnerships and collaboration offer businesses a powerful opportunity to accelerate growth, access new markets, and leverage complementary strengths. By identifying suitable partners, fostering mutually beneficial relationships, and executing strategic initiatives, businesses can unlock new avenues for expansion and achieve their growth objectives more effectively and efficiently. Embrace the potential of strategic partnerships as a key driver of growth and innovation in your business journey.

~~~~~~~~~~~~~~~~~~~~~~~~~~~~~~~~~~~
~~~~~~~~~~~~~~~~~~~~~~~~~~~~~~~~~~~

12.3 Diversification and Innovation Strategies

Diversification and innovation are essential components of a successful growth strategy for businesses looking to expand their market reach and stay ahead of the competition. In this chapter, we delve into the importance of diversification and innovation and provide insights into effective strategies for implementation.

1. Understanding Diversification:

- **Product Diversification:** Expand your product or service offerings to cater to different customer needs, preferences, or market segments. Explore opportunities to introduce new product lines, variants, or extensions that complement your existing offerings.

- **Market Diversification:** Enter new geographic markets, industry sectors, or customer demographics to reduce reliance on a single market or customer segment. Diversifying your market presence can help mitigate risks and capitalize on growth opportunities in untapped areas.

2. Benefits of Diversification:

- **Risk Reduction:** Diversification spreads risk across multiple products, markets, or business lines, reducing reliance on any single source of revenue or market segment.

- **Revenue Growth:** By diversifying your product offerings or market presence, you can tap into new sources of revenue and accelerate business growth.

- **Enhanced Resilience:** Diversification increases business resilience by making your company less vulnerable to market fluctuations, competitive pressures, or industry disruptions.

3. Strategies for Product Innovation:

- **Customer-Centric Innovation:** Focus on understanding customer needs and preferences to drive innovation. Solicit feedback, conduct market research, and use insights to identify opportunities for product enhancements or new solutions.

- **Continuous Improvement:** Foster a culture of innovation within your organization by encouraging creativity, experimentation, and collaboration among employees. Implement processes for collecting, evaluating, and implementing innovative ideas that contribute to product differentiation and customer value.

4. Strategies for Market Innovation:

- **Identifying Emerging Trends:** Stay abreast of industry trends, technological advancements, and market dynamics to identify opportunities for market innovation. Anticipate shifts in customer behavior, preferences, or demands and proactively adapt your business model or offerings to meet evolving needs.

- **Disruptive Innovation:** Challenge traditional industry norms and paradigms by introducing disruptive innovations that redefine market standards or create entirely new market segments. Embrace technology-driven innovations, business model innovations, or process innovations that deliver unique value propositions to customers.

5. Implementing Diversification and Innovation:
- **Strategic Planning:** Develop a comprehensive growth strategy that incorporates diversification and innovation as key pillars. Set clear objectives, allocate resources effectively, and establish timelines and milestones for implementation.

- **Cross-Functional Collaboration:** Foster collaboration and communication across departments, teams, or business units to facilitate cross-pollination of ideas and expertise. Encourage interdisciplinary collaboration to drive innovation and diversification initiatives forward.

6. Case Studies and Success Stories:
- **Highlight successful examples or case studies of businesses that have effectively implemented diversification and innovation strategies to achieve growth and market success.

- **Share real-world experiences, insights, and lessons learned from businesses that have embraced diversification and innovation as core components of their growth strategy.

Diversification and innovation are powerful drivers of growth and competitiveness for businesses seeking to expand their market presence and drive sustainable success. By diversifying product offerings, entering new markets, and fostering a culture of innovation, businesses can unlock new sources of revenue, mitigate risks, and stay ahead of the curve in today's dynamic business landscape. Embrace diversification and innovation as integral components of your growth strategy and propel your business towards continued success and prosperity.

Chapter 13: Financial Management and Planning

13.1 Tracking Financial Performance and Key Metrics

Effective financial management is essential for the growth and sustainability of any business. In this chapter, we delve into the importance of tracking financial performance and highlight key metrics that businesses should monitor to make informed decisions and drive growth.

1. Importance of Tracking Financial Performance:

- **Decision Making:** Regularly tracking financial performance provides insights into the health and profitability of your business, enabling informed decision-making and strategic planning.

- **Performance Evaluation:** Monitoring financial metrics helps evaluate the effectiveness of business strategies, identify areas for improvement, and optimize resource allocation to maximize profitability and efficiency.

- **Investor Confidence:** Transparent financial reporting and performance tracking enhance investor confidence and credibility, facilitating access to capital and fostering business growth.

2. Key Financial Metrics to Track:

- **Revenue Growth:** Monitor revenue trends over time to assess the effectiveness of sales and marketing efforts, identify growth opportunities, and forecast future revenue streams.

- **Profitability Ratios:** Track profitability ratios such as gross profit margin, net profit margin, and operating profit margin to evaluate the efficiency of operations and measure overall profitability.

- **Cash Flow Management:** Monitor cash flow metrics such as cash flow from operations, investing, and financing activities to ensure sufficient liquidity for day-to-day operations, investments, and debt obligations.

- **Working Capital Management:** Assess working capital metrics such as current ratio, quick ratio, and days sales outstanding (DSO) to manage liquidity, optimize inventory levels, and maintain healthy cash flow.

- **Debt Management:** Monitor debt-related metrics such as debt-to-equity ratio, interest coverage ratio, and debt service coverage ratio to assess leverage, debt repayment capacity, and financial stability.

3. Tools and Systems for Financial Tracking:

- **Accounting Software:** Utilize accounting software such as QuickBooks, Xero, or FreshBooks to track income, expenses, and financial transactions in real-time, generate financial reports, and streamline financial management processes.

- **Financial Dashboards:** Implement financial dashboards or reporting tools that provide a snapshot of key financial metrics, KPIs, and performance indicators to facilitate quick decision-making and performance monitoring.

- **Budgeting and Forecasting Tools:** Use budgeting and forecasting software to create financial forecasts, model different scenarios, and track actual performance against budgeted targets to identify variances and adjust strategies accordingly.

4. Financial Reporting and Analysis:

- **Monthly Financial Statements:** Prepare and review monthly financial statements, including income statements, balance sheets, and cash flow statements, to assess financial performance, identify trends, and track progress towards financial goals.

- **Variance Analysis:** Conduct variance analysis to compare actual financial results against budgeted or forecasted figures, identify deviations, and investigate underlying causes to take corrective actions.

- **Benchmarking:** Benchmark financial performance against industry peers or competitors to gauge relative performance, identify areas of competitive advantage or weakness, and set realistic performance targets.

5. Continuous Improvement and Adaptation:

- **Feedback Loop:** Establish a feedback loop for continuous improvement by soliciting feedback from key stakeholders, analyzing financial performance metrics, and identifying opportunities for optimization or innovation.

- **Adaptation to Market Changes:** Stay agile and adaptable in response to changing market conditions, economic trends, or industry disruptions by adjusting financial strategies, revising forecasts, and reallocating resources as needed.

Tracking financial performance and key metrics is fundamental to effective financial management and strategic decision-making for businesses. By monitoring revenue growth, profitability, cash flow, working capital, and debt management metrics, businesses can gain valuable insights into their financial health, identify areas for improvement, and drive sustainable growth and profitability. Embrace the power of financial tracking and analysis as a cornerstone of your business success and take proactive steps to optimize financial performance and achieve your long-term goals.

~~~~~~
~~~~~~

13.2 Budgeting for Growth and Managing Cash Flow

Budgeting for growth and managing cash flow effectively are critical aspects of financial management for businesses seeking to expand and thrive. In this chapter, we explore the importance of budgeting and cash flow management and provide practical strategies for achieving financial stability and fueling growth.

1. Importance of Budgeting for Growth:
- **Strategic Planning:** Budgeting enables businesses to set financial goals, allocate resources, and prioritize investments to support growth initiatives and strategic objectives.

- **Resource Allocation:** By establishing a budget, businesses can allocate funds strategically to key areas such as marketing, research and development, infrastructure, and talent acquisition to drive growth and innovation.

- **Performance Monitoring:** Budgets serve as benchmarks for monitoring financial performance, tracking variances, and identifying opportunities for cost optimization or revenue enhancement to achieve growth targets.

2. Components of a Growth-Oriented Budget:
- **Revenue Projections:** Forecast future revenue streams based on historical performance, market trends, and growth projections to establish realistic revenue targets and inform sales and marketing strategies.

- **Operating Expenses:** Estimate operating expenses such as salaries, utilities, rent, supplies, and marketing expenses to ensure adequate funding for day-to-day operations and growth initiatives.
- **Capital Expenditures:** Allocate funds for capital expenditures such as equipment purchases, technology investments, facility upgrades, and infrastructure improvements to support expansion and innovation.

- **Contingency Planning:** Set aside reserves or contingency funds to address unexpected expenses, mitigate risks, and maintain financial flexibility during periods of uncertainty or economic downturns.

3. Strategies for Managing Cash Flow:

- **Cash Flow Forecasting:** Develop cash flow forecasts to project future cash inflows and outflows, identify potential cash shortfalls or surpluses, and plan accordingly to ensure sufficient liquidity for operating expenses, debt payments, and growth investments.

- **Working Capital Management:** Optimize working capital management by streamlining accounts receivable, accounts payable, and inventory management processes to improve cash flow efficiency, reduce financing costs, and enhance liquidity.

- **Debt Management:** Evaluate debt obligations, interest rates, and repayment schedules to manage debt effectively, minimize interest expenses, and maintain healthy debt-to-equity ratios to support growth and financial stability.

4. Cash Flow Improvement Strategies:

- **Accounts Receivable Management:** Accelerate accounts receivable collections by implementing policies such as offering discounts for early payments, sending timely invoices, and following up on overdue payments to improve cash flow.

- **Accounts Payable Optimization:** Negotiate favorable payment terms with suppliers, vendors, and creditors to extend payment deadlines without incurring penalties or interest charges, preserving cash flow for growth initiatives.

- **Inventory Optimization:** Optimize inventory levels by implementing just-in-time (JIT) inventory management practices, minimizing excess inventory carrying costs, and optimizing inventory turnover ratios to free up working capital and improve cash flow.

5. Continuous Monitoring and Adjustment:

- **Regular Review:** Monitor actual financial performance against budgeted targets on a regular basis, analyze variances, and identify areas for improvement or corrective action to stay on track towards achieving growth objectives.

- **Scenario Planning:** Conduct scenario analysis to assess the impact of various economic, market, or operational scenarios on cash flow, profitability, and financial health, and develop contingency plans to mitigate risks and capitalize on opportunities.

Budgeting for growth and managing cash flow effectively are essential components of financial management for businesses seeking to expand and thrive. By developing growth-oriented budgets, implementing strategies for managing cash flow, and continuously monitoring financial performance, businesses can achieve financial stability, fuel growth initiatives, and position themselves for long-term success and sustainability in today's competitive business landscape. Embrace the power of budgeting and cash flow management as strategic tools for driving growth and achieving your business goals.

~~~~~~~~~~~~~~~~~~~~~~~~
~~~~~~~~~~~~~~~~~~~~~~~~

13.3 Seeking Additional Funding for Expansion

Expanding a business often requires additional capital to fuel growth initiatives, invest in infrastructure, and seize new opportunities. In this chapter, we explore strategies for seeking additional funding to support expansion efforts and drive business growth.

1. Assessing Funding Needs:

- **Identify Growth Opportunities:** Evaluate potential expansion opportunities, such as launching new products, entering new markets, or scaling operations, and estimate the financial resources required to pursue these initiatives effectively.

- **Forecast Financial Requirements:** Develop financial projections and cash flow forecasts to estimate funding needs over the short, medium, and long term, taking into account anticipated growth rates, investment timelines, and capital expenditure requirements.

2. Types of Funding Options:

- **Equity Financing:** Raise capital by selling ownership stakes in the company to investors, venture capitalists, or angel investors in exchange for equity. Equity financing provides access to funds without incurring debt obligations but involves diluting ownership and sharing control of the business.

- **Debt Financing:** Obtain loans, lines of credit, or other debt instruments from banks, financial institutions, or alternative lenders to finance expansion projects. Debt financing allows businesses to retain full ownership and control but requires repayment of principal and interest over time.

- **Alternative Financing:** Explore alternative funding sources such as crowdfunding, peer-to-peer lending, or revenue-based financing to access capital from a diverse range of investors or lenders outside traditional banking channels.

3. Developing a Funding Strategy:

- **Align Funding Sources with Business Goals:** Evaluate the pros and cons of different funding options based on your business objectives, risk tolerance, and growth plans. Choose funding sources that align with your long-term vision and strategic priorities.

- **Diversify Funding Mix:** Consider diversifying your funding sources to spread risk and minimize dependence on any single source of capital. Combine equity and debt financing, as well as alternative funding sources, to create a balanced funding mix that meets your financial needs.

4. Preparing for Funding Rounds:

- **Business Plan and Financial Projections:** Develop a comprehensive business plan and financial projections that articulate your growth strategy, market opportunity, competitive advantage, and potential returns for investors. Provide realistic revenue forecasts, expense estimates, and investment requirements to demonstrate the viability and scalability of your business model.

- **Due Diligence and Documentation:** Prepare due diligence materials, including financial statements, legal documents, and corporate governance documents, to facilitate investor scrutiny and decision-making. Ensure all regulatory and compliance requirements are met and documentation is accurate and up to date.

5. Navigating the Funding Process:

- **Identifying Potential Investors:** Research and identify potential investors or lenders who have experience and interest in your industry, market segment, or growth stage. Network with industry contacts, attend investor events, and leverage online platforms to connect with potential funding partners.

- **Pitching and Negotiation:** Develop a compelling pitch deck and presentation to articulate your business opportunity, value proposition, competitive advantage, and investment thesis to potential investors. Negotiate terms and conditions that are favorable to both parties while safeguarding the interests of your business and existing stakeholders.

6. Post-Funding Management:

- **Effective Capital Deployment:** Deploy capital efficiently and effectively towards growth initiatives outlined in your business plan, ensuring alignment with strategic priorities and maximizing return on investment.

- **Investor Relations:** Maintain transparent and proactive communication with investors, providing regular updates on business performance, milestones achieved, and growth trajectory. Build trust and confidence by demonstrating progress towards stated goals and delivering on commitments.

Seeking additional funding for expansion is a crucial step in scaling your business and realizing its full potential. By assessing funding needs, exploring various funding options, developing a funding strategy, preparing for funding rounds, navigating the funding process effectively, and managing post-funding relationships, businesses can secure the capital needed to fuel growth initiatives and achieve their strategic objectives. Embrace the funding journey as an opportunity to attract strategic partners, accelerate expansion, and position your business for long-term success and sustainability in today's competitive marketplace.

~~~~~~~~~~~~~~~~~~~~~~
~~~~~~~~~~~~~~~~~~~~~~

14.1 Scaling Up Marketing Efforts and Campaigns

As your business expands, scaling up your marketing efforts becomes essential to reach new customers, increase brand visibility, and drive growth. In this chapter, we explore strategies for scaling up marketing campaigns effectively to support your business's expansion objectives.

1. Assessing Marketing Needs:

- **Market Analysis:** Conduct a thorough analysis of your target market, including customer demographics, preferences, and behaviors, to identify opportunities for expansion and refine your marketing strategies accordingly.

- **Competitive Analysis:** Evaluate competitor marketing strategies, positioning, and messaging to identify gaps, differentiation opportunities, and areas where you can leverage your strengths to gain a competitive advantage.

2. Developing a Scalable Marketing Strategy:

- **Clear Objectives:** Define clear and measurable marketing objectives aligned with your business goals, such as increasing brand awareness, generating leads, driving sales, or expanding market share.

- **Target Audience Segmentation:** Segment your target audience based on demographic, psychographic, or behavioral criteria to tailor marketing messages, offers, and channels to specific customer segments and maximize relevance and effectiveness.

- **Multichannel Approach:** Implement a multichannel marketing approach that leverages a mix of online and offline channels, including digital marketing, social media, email marketing, content marketing, search engine optimization (SEO), paid advertising, events, and direct mail, to reach and engage target audiences across multiple touchpoints.

3. Scaling Up Marketing Campaigns:

- **Investment in Technology:** Invest in marketing automation tools, customer relationship management (CRM) systems, analytics platforms, and other marketing technologies to streamline processes, improve efficiency, and scale campaigns effectively.

- **Content Development:** Develop high-quality, engaging content tailored to different stages of the customer journey and across various marketing channels to attract, educate, and convert prospects into customers.

- **Scalable Advertising Strategies:** Implement scalable advertising strategies, such as pay-per-click (PPC) advertising, display advertising, remarketing, and programmatic advertising, to reach targeted audiences at scale and optimize campaign performance based on real-time data and insights.

4. Measurement and Optimization:

- **Key Performance Indicators (KPIs):** Define key performance indicators (KPIs) and metrics to track the effectiveness of your marketing efforts, such as website traffic, conversion rates, lead generation, customer acquisition cost (CAC), return on investment (ROI), and customer lifetime value (CLV).

- **Data Analysis:** Use data analytics and reporting tools to analyze campaign performance, identify trends, patterns, and areas for improvement, and make data-driven decisions to optimize marketing strategies and maximize ROI.

- **Continuous Testing and Iteration:** Adopt a culture of continuous testing and optimization by experimenting with different marketing tactics, messaging, offers, and audience segments, and iterating based on performance insights to improve campaign effectiveness over time.

5. Scaling Up Marketing Teams and Resources:

- **Team Expansion:** Scale up your marketing team by hiring additional staff, contractors, or agencies with expertise in areas such as digital marketing, content creation, social media management, analytics, and advertising to support increased workload and campaign complexity.

- **Training and Development:** Provide ongoing training, education, and professional development opportunities to your marketing team to keep them abreast of industry trends, best practices, and emerging technologies, and empower them to execute scalable marketing strategies effectively.

6. Case Studies and Success Stories:

- **Highlight successful examples or case studies of businesses that have effectively scaled up their marketing efforts and campaigns to achieve business growth and market success.

- **Share real-world experiences, insights, and lessons learned from businesses that have embraced scalable marketing strategies and tactics to drive customer acquisition, increase brand awareness, and generate revenue.

Scaling up marketing efforts and campaigns is essential for businesses seeking to expand their market reach, attract new customers, and drive growth. By developing a scalable marketing strategy, leveraging technology and automation, implementing scalable advertising strategies, measuring and optimizing campaign performance, and scaling up marketing teams and resources, businesses can effectively reach target audiences, generate leads, and achieve their growth objectives. Embrace scalable marketing as a strategic tool for driving business growth and staying ahead in today's competitive marketplace.

~~~~~~~~~~~~~~~~~
~~~~~~~~~~~~~~~~~

14.2 Building Customer Loyalty and Retention Strategies

While acquiring new customers is essential for business growth, retaining existing customers is equally important for long-term success and sustainability. In this chapter, we explore strategies for building customer loyalty and implementing retention strategies to foster strong relationships and maximize customer lifetime value.

1. Understanding the Importance of Customer Loyalty:

- **Lifetime Value:** Recognize the value of loyal customers who make repeat purchases, provide valuable feedback, and serve as brand advocates, contributing significantly to the overall revenue and profitability of your business.

- **Reduced Acquisition Costs:** Understand that retaining existing customers is often more cost-effective than acquiring new ones, as it involves fewer marketing expenses and resources, making it a strategic priority for businesses seeking sustainable growth.

2. Developing Customer Loyalty Programs:

- **Reward Systems:** Implement customer loyalty programs that reward customers for their repeat purchases, referrals, and engagement with your brand through incentives such as discounts, exclusive offers, loyalty points, or VIP perks.

- **Personalization:** Tailor loyalty programs to individual customer preferences, behaviors, and purchase histories to deliver personalized rewards and experiences that resonate with their interests and needs.

3. Providing Exceptional Customer Service:

- **Responsive Communication:** Prioritize prompt and responsive communication with customers across various touchpoints, including phone, email, chat, and social media, to address inquiries, resolve issues, and provide assistance in a timely manner.

- **Empathy and Understanding:** Demonstrate empathy and understanding towards customer concerns and feedback, actively listening to their needs, and taking proactive steps to exceed their expectations and enhance their overall experience.

4. Creating Engaging Content and Experiences:

- **Content Marketing:** Develop high-quality, relevant content that educates, entertains, and adds value to your customers' lives, positioning your brand as a trusted resource and thought leader in your industry.

- **Interactive Experiences:** Offer interactive experiences such as webinars, workshops, quizzes, or contests that engage customers and encourage active participation, fostering a sense of community and connection with your brand.

5. Implementing Feedback Mechanisms:

- **Surveys and Feedback Forms:** Collect feedback from customers through surveys, feedback forms, or online reviews to gather insights into their satisfaction levels, preferences, and pain points, and use this data to identify areas for improvement and innovation.

- **Custom Sentiment and Metrics:** Track key customer satisfaction metrics such as Net Promoter Score (NPS), Customer Satisfaction Score (CSAT), and Customer Effort Score (CES) to measure loyalty, gauge sentiment, and identify opportunities for enhancement.

6. Leveraging Technology for Customer Engagement:

- **CRM Systems:** Utilize customer relationship management (CRM) systems to centralize customer data, track interactions, and segment customers based on their behavior, preferences, and purchase history, enabling personalized communication and targeted marketing campaigns.

- **Marketing Automation:** Implement marketing automation tools to streamline customer engagement processes, such as email workflows, drip campaigns, and personalized messaging, to deliver timely and relevant communications at scale.

7. Case Studies and Success Stories:

- **Highlight successful examples or case studies of businesses that have effectively built customer loyalty and retention strategies to cultivate long-term relationships and drive business growth.

- **Share real-world experiences, insights, and best practices from businesses that have prioritized customer loyalty and implemented innovative retention strategies to reduce churn, increase customer satisfaction, and boost profitability.

Building customer loyalty and implementing retention strategies are essential components of a successful growth strategy for businesses seeking long-term success and sustainability. By developing customer loyalty programs, providing exceptional customer service, creating engaging content and experiences, implementing feedback mechanisms, leveraging technology for customer engagement, and sharing success stories, businesses can cultivate strong relationships with customers, foster brand loyalty, and maximize customer lifetime value. Embrace customer loyalty as a strategic priority and invest in initiatives that prioritize customer satisfaction and retention to drive sustainable growth and profitability in today's competitive marketplace.

~~~~~~
~~~~~~

14.3 Exploring New Market Segments and Target Audiences

Expanding into new market segments and targeting different audience demographics can unlock significant growth opportunities for businesses. In this chapter, we explore strategies for exploring new market segments and effectively targeting diverse audiences to drive business expansion.

1. Market Segmentation Analysis:

- **Identify Untapped Segments:** Conduct market research to identify potential new market segments that align with your business objectives, such as geographic regions, demographic groups, psychographic profiles, or industry verticals.

- **Segmentation Criteria:** Define segmentation criteria based on factors such as age, gender, income level, lifestyle preferences, purchasing behavior, geographic location, or product usage patterns to segment target audiences effectively.

2. Assessing Market Potential:

- **Market Sizing:** Estimate the size and growth potential of new market segments by analyzing demographic data, market trends, competitive landscape, and consumer preferences to assess market attractiveness and viability.

- **Gap Analysis:** Identify gaps or unmet needs within new market segments that your products or services can address, offering unique value propositions and differentiation opportunities to capture market share.

3. Tailoring Marketing Strategies:

- **Customized Messaging:** Develop tailored marketing messages, value propositions, and positioning statements that resonate with the needs, aspirations, and pain points of new target audiences, addressing their specific concerns and motivations.

- **Localization Strategies:** Customize marketing campaigns, content, and communication channels to suit the cultural, linguistic, and regulatory nuances of different geographic markets, ensuring relevance and effectiveness in engaging local audiences.

4. Testing and Iteration:

- **Pilot Programs:** Launch pilot programs or test campaigns in new market segments to gather feedback, validate assumptions, and refine marketing strategies before scaling up investments and resources.

- **A/B Testing:** Conduct A/B testing of marketing materials, messaging variations, and campaign elements to identify the most effective approaches for reaching and engaging new target audiences, optimizing conversion rates and return on investment.

5. Strategic Partnerships and Alliances:

- **Collaborative Opportunities:** Explore strategic partnerships, alliances, or distribution channels with complementary businesses, industry associations, or influencers in new market segments to leverage existing networks and amplify your reach and credibility.

- **Co-marketing Initiatives:** Collaborate on co-marketing initiatives, joint promotions, or cross-selling opportunities with partners to access their customer base, gain endorsements, and expand brand awareness in new market segments.

6. Data-Driven Decision Making:

- **Market Intelligence:** Leverage data analytics, market research, and customer insights to inform strategic decision-making and prioritize resource allocation in exploring new market segments with the highest growth potential and return on investment.

- **Performance Monitoring:** Track and measure key performance indicators (KPIs) such as customer acquisition costs, conversion rates, customer lifetime value, and market share gains to evaluate the effectiveness of marketing efforts and adjust strategies accordingly.

Exploring new market segments and target audiences presents exciting opportunities for businesses to expand their reach, drive growth, and diversify revenue streams. By conducting market segmentation analysis, assessing market potential, tailoring marketing strategies, testing and iteration, forging strategic partnerships, and leveraging data-driven decision-making, businesses can effectively penetrate new markets, acquire customers, and achieve sustainable business growth. Embrace innovation and adaptability as you explore new frontiers and unlock the full potential of your business in today's dynamic and competitive marketplace.

~~~~~~
~~~~~~

15.1 Identifying Business Risks and Developing Risk Mitigation Plans

Every business faces a variety of risks that can impact its operations, reputation, and financial stability. In this chapter, we explore strategies for identifying potential risks and developing effective risk mitigation plans to safeguard your business against unforeseen challenges.

1. Risk Identification:

- **Internal Risks:** Identify internal risks arising from within your organization, such as operational inefficiencies, human resource issues, financial mismanagement, or technology failures, that could adversely affect business performance.

- **External Risks:** Assess external risks stemming from factors beyond your control, such as economic downturns, regulatory changes, market volatility, competitive pressures, natural disasters, or geopolitical events, that may pose threats to your business continuity.

2. Risk Assessment and Prioritization:

- **Impact Analysis:** Evaluate the potential impact of identified risks on your business objectives, operations, stakeholders, and financial health, considering both the likelihood of occurrence and the magnitude of consequences.

- **Risk Prioritization:** Prioritize risks based on their severity, urgency, and likelihood of occurrence, focusing resources and attention on addressing high-priority risks with the greatest potential impact on your business.

3. Developing Risk Mitigation Plans:

- **Risk Mitigation Strategies:** Develop proactive risk mitigation strategies and contingency plans to mitigate the impact of identified risks and minimize their likelihood of occurrence, such as implementing preventive controls, risk transfer mechanisms, or crisis management protocols.

- **Scenario Planning:** Conduct scenario planning exercises to anticipate and prepare for various risk scenarios, including best-case, worst-case, and most likely outcomes, and develop response strategies to effectively navigate through challenging situations.

4. Risk Monitoring and Management:

- **Continuous Monitoring:** Implement a robust risk monitoring and management framework to continuously monitor and evaluate risks, detect early warning signs, and proactively address emerging threats before they escalate into crises.

- **Regular Reviews:** Conduct regular reviews and assessments of risk mitigation plans, updating them as needed in response to changing business conditions, emerging risks, or lessons learned from past experiences to ensure their effectiveness and relevance over time.

5. Stakeholder Engagement and Communication:

- **Transparent Communication:** Foster open and transparent communication with stakeholders, including employees, customers, suppliers, investors, and regulators, regarding potential risks, mitigation efforts, and crisis response protocols to build trust and confidence in your organization's resilience and preparedness.

- **Employee Training:** Provide comprehensive training and awareness programs to educate employees about potential risks, their roles and responsibilities in risk management, and how to respond effectively to mitigate risks and protect the interests of the business.

6. Continuous Improvement and Adaptation:

- **Learning from Experience:** Embrace a culture of continuous improvement and learning, leveraging insights from past risk events, near misses, or industry benchmarks to refine risk management practices, strengthen controls, and enhance organizational resilience.

- **Agility and Flexibility:** Maintain agility and flexibility in responding to evolving risks and changing business dynamics, adapting risk mitigation plans and strategies as needed to address new challenges and seize emerging opportunities in a rapidly evolving environment.

Identifying business risks and developing effective risk mitigation plans are essential components of proactive risk management and business resilience. By systematically identifying potential risks, assessing their impact and likelihood, developing proactive risk mitigation strategies, monitoring risks continuously, engaging stakeholders, and fostering a culture of continuous improvement and adaptation, businesses can enhance their ability to anticipate, mitigate, and respond to risks effectively, safeguarding their long-term success and sustainability in today's dynamic and uncertain business landscape. Embrace risk management as a strategic imperative and invest in robust risk mitigation practices to protect your business and seize opportunities for growth and innovation with confidence.

~~~~~~~~~~~~~~~~~~~~~~~
~~~~~~~~~~~~~~~~~~~~~~~

15.2 Crisis Management and Contingency Planning

In today's volatile business environment, unforeseen crises can arise at any moment, threatening the stability and continuity of your business. In this chapter, we explore strategies for effective crisis management and contingency planning to help businesses navigate through challenging times and emerge stronger from adversity.

1. Understanding Crisis Scenarios:

- **Identify Potential Crisis Events:** Anticipate and identify potential crisis events that could disrupt your business operations or reputation, such as natural disasters, cyber-attacks, product recalls, supply chain disruptions, financial emergencies, or public relations crises.

- **Assessing Impact:** Evaluate the potential impact of crisis scenarios on your business, including financial losses, operational disruptions, damage to brand reputation, legal liabilities, regulatory penalties, and stakeholder confidence.

2. Developing a Crisis Management Plan:

- **Establish a Crisis Management Team:** Formulate a dedicated crisis management team comprising key decision-makers, department heads, and subject matter experts responsible for overseeing crisis response efforts, coordinating communication, and implementing mitigation measures.

- **Define Roles and Responsibilities:** Clearly define roles, responsibilities, and decision-making authority within the crisis management team, ensuring clarity and accountability in executing crisis response procedures and protocols.

3. Crisis Communication Strategies:

- **Timely Communication:** Establish communication protocols and channels for disseminating timely and accurate information to internal and external stakeholders, including employees, customers, suppliers, investors, media, regulators, and the public, to manage perceptions and mitigate reputational damage.

- **Transparency and Authenticity:** Prioritize transparency, honesty, and authenticity in crisis communication efforts, acknowledging mistakes, addressing concerns, and demonstrating empathy and accountability to build trust and credibility with stakeholders.

4. Implementing Contingency Plans:

- **Risk Mitigation Measures:** Develop contingency plans and risk mitigation measures tailored to specific crisis scenarios, including alternative operational strategies, backup systems, redundant suppliers, insurance coverage, and financial reserves, to minimize the impact of disruptions on business continuity.

- **Business Continuity Planning:** Establish comprehensive business continuity plans outlining procedures for maintaining essential business functions, operations, and services during and after a crisis, ensuring resilience and recovery in the face of adversity.

5. Testing and Exercising:

- **Simulation Exercises:** Conduct regular crisis simulation exercises, tabletop drills, or scenario-based training sessions to test the effectiveness of crisis management plans, evaluate response capabilities, identify gaps, and refine strategies before facing real-life emergencies.

- **Lessons Learned:** Debrief after crisis simulations or actual events to capture lessons learned, best practices, and areas for improvement, incorporating feedback and insights into future crisis management efforts to enhance preparedness and response capabilities.

6. Building Organizational Resilience:

- **Adaptability and Flexibility:** Cultivate a culture of adaptability, agility, and resilience within your organization, empowering employees to respond proactively to changing circumstances, innovate solutions, and collaborate effectively to overcome challenges and bounce back from setbacks.

- **Continuous Improvement:** Foster a mindset of continuous improvement and learning, leveraging experiences from crisis events to refine crisis management processes, strengthen risk mitigation strategies, and enhance organizational preparedness for future challenges.

Crisis management and contingency planning are critical components of business resilience and continuity, enabling organizations to effectively navigate through turbulent times and emerge stronger from adversity. By understanding potential crisis scenarios, developing comprehensive crisis management plans, implementing contingency measures, prioritizing transparent and timely communication, testing response capabilities, and fostering organizational resilience, businesses can mitigate risks, protect stakeholders, and preserve value in the face of unforeseen challenges. Embrace crisis management as a strategic imperative and invest in proactive planning and preparedness to safeguard your business's long-term success and sustainability in today's unpredictable and rapidly evolving business landscape.

~~~~~~
~~~~~~

15.3 Adapting to Market Changes and Competitive Pressures

In the dynamic landscape of business, market changes and competitive pressures are inevitable. This chapter delves into strategies for effectively adapting to market changes and competitive pressures to maintain resilience and drive sustainable growth.

1. Monitoring Market Trends:

- **Stay Informed:** Keep a close eye on market trends, consumer behavior, industry developments, and competitor activities through market research, industry reports, customer feedback, and competitive analysis to identify emerging opportunities and threats.

- **Anticipate Changes:** Proactively anticipate market changes, technological advancements, regulatory shifts, and economic fluctuations that could impact your industry and business operations, preparing contingency plans and strategic responses accordingly.

2. Agility and Flexibility:

- **Embrace Agility:** Cultivate a culture of agility and flexibility within your organization, empowering employees to adapt quickly to changing market dynamics, seize opportunities, and pivot strategies in response to evolving customer needs and competitive pressures.

- **Iterative Approach:** Adopt an iterative approach to strategy formulation and execution, allowing for experimentation, learning, and course correction based on real-time feedback and market insights to stay ahead of the curve.

3. Innovation and Differentiation:

- **Continuous Innovation:** Foster a culture of innovation and creativity, encouraging employees to generate new ideas, products, services, or business models that address unmet customer needs, disrupt existing markets, and create sustainable competitive advantages.

- **Value Proposition:** Differentiate your offerings from competitors by delivering unique value propositions, superior quality, innovative features, personalized experiences, or exceptional customer service that resonate with target audiences and set your brand apart in the marketplace.

4. Strategic Partnerships and Collaborations:

- **Forge Alliances:** Explore strategic partnerships, alliances, or collaborations with complementary businesses, startups, research institutions, or industry disruptors to leverage their expertise, resources, or distribution channels and capitalize on synergies for mutual growth and competitiveness.

- **Co-opetition:** Embrace a spirit of co-opetition with competitors, where appropriate, by collaborating on industry standards, joint ventures, or consortia initiatives to address common challenges, drive industry innovation, and create win-win outcomes for all stakeholders.

5. Customer-Centric Approach:

- **Customer Insights:** Listen attentively to customer feedback, preferences, and pain points, leveraging customer insights to tailor your offerings, improve service delivery, and enhance customer experiences that drive satisfaction, loyalty, and advocacy in the face of competitive pressures.
- **Agile Response:** Respond swiftly to changing customer demands, preferences, and expectations, adapting product features, pricing strategies, marketing campaigns, or distribution channels to meet evolving market needs and maintain a competitive edge.

6. Continuous Learning and Improvement:

- **Market Intelligence:** Invest in market intelligence capabilities to gather actionable insights, competitive intelligence, and industry benchmarks that inform strategic decision-making, fuel innovation, and guide resource allocation to maximize competitive advantage.

- **Organizational Learning:** Foster a learning culture that encourages continuous improvement, knowledge sharing, and cross-functional collaboration, enabling employees to develop new skills, stay abreast of market trends, and adapt to evolving business environments effectively.

Adapting to market changes and competitive pressures is essential for business survival and growth in today's dynamic and hypercompetitive marketplace. By monitoring market trends, embracing agility and flexibility, fostering innovation and differentiation, forging strategic partnerships, adopting a customer-centric approach, and prioritizing continuous learning and improvement, businesses can effectively navigate through uncertainty, seize opportunities, and maintain competitiveness in the face of evolving market dynamics. Embrace change as an opportunity for growth and leverage your adaptive capabilities to thrive in an ever-changing business landscape.

∾∾∾∾∾∾∾∾∾∾∾∾∾∾∾∾∾∾∾∾∾

16.1 Incorporating Environmental and Social Responsibility

In today's socially conscious world, businesses are increasingly expected to operate with a sense of responsibility towards the environment and society. This chapter explores strategies for incorporating environmental and social responsibility into your business practices to drive sustainability and long-term success.

1. Environmental Sustainability:

- **Assess Environmental Impact:** Conduct a thorough assessment of your business operations to identify areas where you can reduce environmental impact, such as energy consumption, waste generation, water usage, and carbon emissions.

- **Implement Eco-Friendly Practices:** Implement eco-friendly practices and initiatives, such as recycling programs, energy-efficient technologies, sustainable sourcing, and green packaging, to minimize your carbon footprint and conserve natural resources.

2. Social Responsibility:

- **Stakeholder Engagement:** Engage with stakeholders, including employees, customers, suppliers, local communities, and NGOs, to understand their social concerns and priorities, and incorporate their feedback into your business practices.

- **Corporate Philanthropy:** Allocate resources towards corporate philanthropy initiatives, such as community development projects, educational programs, healthcare initiatives, or disaster relief efforts, to give back to society and make a positive impact on the communities you serve.

3. Ethical Business Practices:

- **Ethical Sourcing:** Adopt ethical sourcing practices by ensuring fair labor practices, humane treatment of workers, and responsible sourcing of materials and ingredients, avoiding suppliers with questionable ethical standards or human rights violations.

- **Transparency and Accountability:** Practice transparency and accountability in your business operations by disclosing information about your supply chain, labor practices, environmental impact, and social initiatives to build trust and credibility with stakeholders.

4. Diversity and Inclusion:

- **Promote Diversity:** Foster a culture of diversity and inclusion within your organization by promoting equal opportunities, hiring practices, and workplace policies that respect and celebrate differences in gender, race, ethnicity, age, sexual orientation, and physical abilities.

- **Diverse Suppliers:** Partner with diverse suppliers and vendors from underrepresented communities to promote economic inclusion and support small businesses owned by women, minorities, veterans, or individuals with disabilities.

5. Impact Measurement and Reporting:

- **Key Performance Indicators:** Define key performance indicators (KPIs) and metrics to measure your environmental and social impact, such as carbon footprint, energy efficiency, waste reduction, employee diversity, community engagement, and philanthropic contributions.

- **Sustainability Reporting:** Publish annual sustainability reports or corporate social responsibility (CSR) disclosures to communicate your environmental and social performance, goals, achievements, and challenges transparently to stakeholders and demonstrate your commitment to sustainability.

6. Continuous Improvement:

- **Stakeholder Feedback:** Solicit feedback from stakeholders on your environmental and social initiatives, and use their input to identify areas for improvement, address concerns, and enhance the effectiveness of your sustainability efforts.

- **Adaptive Management:** Embrace adaptive management principles to continuously refine and adapt your environmental and social responsibility strategies in response to changing stakeholder expectations, regulatory requirements, and societal needs.

Incorporating environmental and social responsibility into your business practices is not only a moral imperative but also a strategic imperative for long-term success and sustainability. By prioritizing environmental sustainability, social responsibility, ethical business practices, diversity and inclusion, impact measurement, and continuous improvement, businesses can create shared value for stakeholders, mitigate risks, enhance reputation, and contribute positively to the well-being of the planet and society. Embrace sustainability as a core business principle and leverage your influence and resources to drive positive change in the world while achieving your business goals and objectives.

~~~~~~~~~~
~~~~~~~~~~

16.2 Creating a Positive Workplace Culture and Employee Well-being

A positive workplace culture and employee well-being are fundamental pillars of a sustainable and successful business. In this chapter, we delve into strategies for fostering a supportive and inclusive work environment that promotes employee happiness, engagement, and overall well-being.

1. Cultivating a Supportive Culture:

- **Clear Values and Mission:** Define clear values and a compelling mission statement that aligns with your company's goals and resonates with employees, providing a sense of purpose and direction that inspires commitment and engagement.

- **Open Communication:** Foster open communication channels that encourage transparency, feedback, and dialogue between management and employees, creating a culture of trust, collaboration, and shared ownership in decision-making processes.

2. Prioritizing Employee Well-being:

- **Work-Life Balance:** Promote work-life balance by offering flexible work arrangements, remote work options, and paid time off policies that enable employees to manage personal responsibilities, pursue interests outside of work, and recharge for optimal performance.

- **Mental Health Support:** Provide resources and support for mental health and stress management, such as employee assistance programs, counseling services, mindfulness training, and wellness initiatives, to help employees cope with work-related stressors and maintain mental well-being.

3. Empowering and Developing Employees:

- **Employee Empowerment:** Empower employees by delegating authority, encouraging autonomy, and providing opportunities for skill development, career advancement, and professional growth, fostering a sense of ownership, mastery, and purpose in their roles.

- **Training and Development:** Invest in training and development programs that equip employees with the knowledge, skills, and tools needed to succeed in their roles, adapt to changing job requirements, and pursue career aspirations within the organization.

4. Recognizing and Rewarding Contributions:

- **Employee Recognition:** Implement employee recognition programs and initiatives to acknowledge and celebrate individual and team achievements, contributions, and milestones, reinforcing a culture of appreciation, motivation, and pride in accomplishments.

- **Incentive Programs:** Design incentive programs, bonuses, and rewards tied to performance metrics, key objectives, or exemplary behaviors, incentivizing high performance, innovation, and alignment with organizational goals.

5. Promoting Diversity and Inclusion:
- **Diverse and Inclusive Environment:** Foster a diverse and inclusive workplace culture that values and respects differences in gender, race, ethnicity, age, sexual orientation, religion, and background, creating a sense of belonging and equity for all employees.

- **Diversity Training:** Provide diversity training and awareness programs to educate employees on unconscious bias, cultural competence, and inclusive leadership practices, fostering empathy, understanding, and collaboration across diverse teams.

6. Soliciting Employee Feedback and Engagement:
- **Employee Surveys:** Conduct regular employee surveys, pulse checks, or feedback sessions to gather insights, opinions, and suggestions from employees on workplace satisfaction, engagement levels, and areas for improvement, demonstrating a commitment to listening and responsiveness.

- **Action Planning:** Act on employee feedback by developing action plans and initiatives to address identified concerns, implement meaningful changes, and enhance the employee experience, fostering a culture of continuous improvement and responsiveness to employee needs.

Creating a positive workplace culture and prioritizing employee well-being are essential strategies for building a sustainable business that thrives in the long term. By cultivating a supportive culture, prioritizing employee well-being, empowering and developing employees, recognizing contributions, promoting diversity and inclusion, and soliciting employee feedback and engagement, businesses can foster a motivated, engaged, and resilient workforce that drives innovation, productivity, and organizational success. Invest in your employees as your most valuable asset, and cultivate a workplace where they feel valued, respected, and empowered to reach their full potential while contributing to the overall success and sustainability of your business.

~~~~~~~~~~~~~~~~~~~~~~~~~~~~~~~~~~~~~~~
~~~~~~~~~~~~~~~~~~~~~~~~~~~~~~~~~~~~~~~

16.3 Community Engagement and Corporate Social Responsibility

Community engagement and corporate social responsibility (CSR) are integral components of building a sustainable business that creates positive impact beyond financial returns. In this chapter, we explore strategies for effectively engaging with communities and fulfilling social responsibilities to drive meaningful change and foster long-term sustainability.

1. Community Needs Assessment:
- **Identify Community Needs:** Conduct a thorough assessment of community needs, challenges, and priorities through stakeholder consultations, surveys, and partnerships with local organizations, gaining insights into areas where your business can make a meaningful impact.

2. Stakeholder Collaboration:
- **Collaborative Partnerships:** Forge collaborative partnerships with local governments, non-profit organizations, community groups, and other stakeholders to address community needs, leverage collective resources, and maximize impact through coordinated efforts.

- **Engagement Platforms:** Establish platforms for ongoing dialogue and engagement with community stakeholders, including town hall meetings, community forums, advisory councils, and volunteer opportunities, fostering transparency, trust, and mutual understanding.

3. Social Impact Initiatives:

- **Education and Skill Development:** Support education and skill development programs in local communities through initiatives such as scholarships, vocational training, mentoring, and job placement assistance, empowering individuals to enhance their livelihoods and career prospects.

- **Health and Wellness:** Promote health and wellness initiatives, such as healthcare clinics, wellness workshops, nutrition programs, and fitness activities, to improve access to healthcare services and promote well-being among community members.

4. Environmental Sustainability:

- **Environmental Conservation:** Implement environmental sustainability projects, such as tree planting drives, waste management programs, clean energy initiatives, and water conservation efforts, to protect natural resources, mitigate environmental degradation, and enhance community resilience.

- **Eco-Friendly Practices:** Integrate eco-friendly practices into your business operations, supply chain, and products/services to minimize environmental impact and promote sustainable consumption and production patterns within the community.

5. Philanthropy and Charitable Giving:

- **Financial Contributions:** Allocate funds towards philanthropic initiatives, charitable giving, and community grants that support local causes, address pressing social issues, and improve the quality of life for vulnerable populations, demonstrating a commitment to social responsibility and corporate citizenship.

- **Employee Volunteerism:** Encourage employee volunteerism and community service by offering paid volunteer days, organizing group volunteer activities, and matching employee donations to charitable organizations, fostering a culture of giving back and civic engagement among staff members.

6. Impact Measurement and Reporting:

- **Metrics and Indicators:** Define key performance indicators (KPIs) and metrics to measure the social impact of your community engagement and CSR initiatives, such as lives impacted, beneficiaries served, volunteer hours contributed, and funds invested in social programs.

- **Sustainability Reporting:** Publish annual CSR reports or sustainability disclosures to transparently communicate your social impact goals, progress, challenges, and outcomes to stakeholders, demonstrating accountability and driving continuous improvement in your community engagement efforts.

Community engagement and corporate social responsibility are crucial for sustainable businesses, creating positive change and adding value to society. By actively engaging with communities, collaborating with stakeholders, and supporting social impact initiatives, businesses strengthen their reputation, brand loyalty, and long-term sustainability. Embrace your role as a responsible corporate citizen to make a meaningful difference and leave a positive legacy.

17.1 Staying Compliant with Changing Regulations and Laws

Navigating the complex landscape of legal and regulatory requirements is crucial for the sustained success and growth of any business, especially in the Indian context. In this chapter, we explore strategies for staying compliant with changing regulations and laws, with a particular focus on data privacy compliance within India.

1. Regulatory Awareness:

- **Monitor Indian Data Protection Laws:** Stay informed about Indian data protection laws and regulations, particularly the Personal Data Protection Bill (PDPB) and the existing framework under the Information Technology (Reasonable Security Practices and Procedures and Sensitive Personal Data or Information) Rules, 2011, to ensure compliance with evolving data privacy requirements.

2. Compliance Management:

- **Conduct Data Privacy Assessments:** Conduct regular data privacy assessments and audits of your business processes, systems, and practices to identify areas of non-compliance with Indian data protection laws, assess data security risks, and implement remedial measures to mitigate legal and regulatory risks.

- **Employee Training on Data Privacy:** Provide comprehensive training programs for employees on data privacy laws, policies, and best practices, emphasizing the importance of safeguarding personal data, understanding individual rights, and complying with data protection principles in their day-to-day activities.

3. Data Protection and Privacy:

- **Data Localization Compliance:** Ensure compliance with data localization requirements under Indian law, including restrictions on cross-border transfer of sensitive personal data, by storing and processing personal data of Indian residents within servers located in India or through approved mechanisms for data transfer.

- **Data Subject Rights:** Establish mechanisms for responding to data subject requests, such as access, rectification, erasure, and portability, in accordance with the rights conferred to individuals under Indian data protection laws, ensuring transparency and accountability in handling personal data.

4. Proactive Data Security Measures:

- **Data Security Policies and Procedures:** Develop and implement robust data security policies, procedures, and technical safeguards to protect personal data from unauthorized access, disclosure, alteration, and destruction, aligning with the security requirements prescribed by Indian data protection laws.

- **Incident Response Planning:** Prepare incident response plans and procedures for addressing data breaches, security incidents, and privacy violations in compliance with the mandatory breach notification requirements under Indian data protection laws, ensuring timely reporting to regulatory authorities and affected individuals.

5. Vendor Management and Due Diligence:
- **Vendor Compliance Assessment:** Conduct due diligence on third-party vendors, service providers, and data processors to assess their data protection practices, security controls, and compliance with Indian data privacy laws before engaging in data processing activities or sharing personal data with external parties.

- **Contractual Safeguards:** Incorporate contractual provisions, data processing agreements, and indemnification clauses into vendor contracts to ensure compliance with Indian data protection laws, define data protection responsibilities, and mitigate legal and regulatory risks associated with third-party data processing.

6. Regulatory Engagement and Advocacy:
- **Engage with Regulatory Authorities:** Establish channels for communication and engagement with regulatory authorities, such as the Data Protection Authority (DPA) established under the PDPB, to seek guidance, clarification, and interpretation on data privacy issues, compliance requirements, and regulatory expectations.

- **Industry Advocacy Initiatives:** Participate in industry associations, forums, and advocacy groups focused on data privacy and cybersecurity to stay updated on emerging trends, share best practices, and collaborate on advocacy efforts to influence policy development and regulatory frameworks in India.

Conclusion: Staying compliant with data privacy regulations in India is crucial for businesses to protect individual privacy rights, maintain trust with customers, and avoid legal penalties. Prioritize regulatory awareness, compliance management, data protection, proactive security measures, vendor management, and regulatory engagement. Embrace data privacy as a strategic imperative, investing in resources, expertise, and technology to ensure regulatory compliance and foster a culture of trust for sustainable growth and success in the Indian market.

~~~~~~~~~~~~~~~~~~~~~~
~~~~~~~~~~~~~~~~~~~~~~

17.2 Updating Business Licenses and Permits

Ensuring compliance with licensing and permit requirements is essential for the lawful operation of your business. In this chapter, we explore the importance of updating business licenses and permits to remain compliant with regulatory standards and avoid legal risks.

1. Reviewing Current Licenses and Permits:

- **Assess Existing Licenses:** Conduct a thorough review of all current business licenses, permits, and regulatory approvals held by your company, ensuring they are up to date, valid, and compliant with relevant laws and regulations.

- **Identify Renewal Deadlines:** Identify renewal deadlines and expiration dates for each license and permit to prevent lapses in compliance and avoid potential penalties or disruptions to business operations.

2. Understanding Regulatory Changes:

- **Monitor Regulatory Updates:** Stay informed about changes in licensing requirements, regulatory standards, and industry-specific regulations that may impact your business, including updates to zoning laws, health and safety regulations, environmental permits, and industry certifications.

- **Engage with Regulatory Authorities:** Establish communication channels with regulatory authorities and government agencies responsible for issuing licenses and permits, seeking guidance and clarification on compliance requirements and procedural changes.

3. Updating License Applications and Documentation:

- **Submit Renewal Applications:** Prepare and submit renewal applications for business licenses and permits well in advance of expiration dates, providing all required documentation, fees, and supporting materials to regulatory authorities to facilitate prompt processing and approval.

- **Amendments and Modifications:** Assess the need for any amendments or modifications to existing licenses or permits based on changes in business activities, operational scope, or regulatory requirements, submitting necessary applications and documentation to regulatory agencies as needed.

4. Compliance Audits and Recordkeeping:

- **Conduct Compliance Audits:** Conduct periodic audits of licensing and permit compliance, reviewing documentation, records, and operational practices to ensure adherence to regulatory requirements and identify any areas of non-compliance or potential risks.

- **Maintain Accurate Records:** Maintain accurate and up-to-date records of all business licenses, permits, approvals, and regulatory correspondence, organizing documentation in a centralized system for easy access and retrieval during regulatory inspections or audits.

5. Seeking Legal Counsel and Advisory Services:

- **Consult Legal Experts:** Seek guidance and advice from legal experts, attorneys, or regulatory consultants with expertise in licensing and regulatory compliance, especially when navigating complex regulatory frameworks or addressing specific compliance challenges.

- **Utilize Advisory Services:** Engage advisory services or compliance management solutions that offer assistance with license tracking, renewal reminders, compliance monitoring, and regulatory updates to streamline the process of managing business licenses and permits.

Updating business licenses and permits is a critical aspect of maintaining regulatory compliance and ensuring the legality of your business operations. By reviewing current licenses, understanding regulatory changes, updating license applications and documentation, conducting compliance audits, and seeking legal counsel or advisory services when needed, businesses can mitigate legal risks, avoid regulatory penalties, and demonstrate a commitment to operating ethically and responsibly within the regulatory framework. Make compliance a priority and invest resources in staying updated and organized to navigate the licensing and permitting process effectively, safeguarding the legitimacy and reputation of your business in the marketplace.

~~~~~~~~~~~~~~~~~~~~~~~~~~~~~~~~~~~~~~
~~~~~~~~~~~~~~~~~~~~~~~~~~~~~~~~~~~~~~

17.3 Protecting Intellectual Property Rights

Intellectual property (IP) rights are invaluable assets for businesses, providing legal protection for inventions, creations, and innovations. In this chapter, we delve into the importance of protecting intellectual property rights to safeguard your competitive advantage and mitigate risks.

1. Identifying Intellectual Property Assets:

- **Inventory IP Assets:** Conduct a comprehensive inventory of your intellectual property assets, including patents, trademarks, copyrights, trade secrets, and proprietary technologies, identifying key assets that contribute to the value and uniqueness of your business.

2. Securing Legal Protection:

- **Patent Protection:** File patent applications to protect inventions, processes, and technological innovations from unauthorized use, reproduction, or distribution, securing exclusive rights to commercialize and monetize your inventions for a specified period.

- **Trademark Registration:** Register trademarks for company names, logos, slogans, and product/service identifiers to establish brand identity, prevent brand dilution, and protect against trademark infringement or counterfeiting in the marketplace.

- **Copyright Registration:** Obtain copyright protection for original works of authorship, such as literary works, artistic creations, software code, and digital content, preserving exclusive rights to reproduce, distribute, display, and perform copyrighted works.

- **Trade Secret Protection:** Implement trade secret protection measures, such as confidentiality agreements, non-disclosure agreements (NDAs), and restricted access controls, to safeguard proprietary information, formulas, processes, and business strategies from unauthorized disclosure or misappropriation.

3. Monitoring and Enforcement:

- **Monitor IP Infringement:** Vigilantly monitor the marketplace for potential infringements of your intellectual property rights, including unauthorized use, imitation, or misappropriation by competitors, counterfeiters, or unauthorized third parties.

- **Enforce Legal Rights:** Take proactive measures to enforce your intellectual property rights through cease-and-desist letters, litigation, or administrative actions against infringers, seeking legal remedies, damages, injunctions, or other relief to protect your interests and deter future infringements.

4. Licensing and Commercialization:

- **Licensing Agreements:** Enter into licensing agreements with third parties to monetize your intellectual property assets, granting permission for others to use, manufacture, or distribute your patented inventions, trademarked brands, copyrighted works, or trade secrets in exchange for royalties or licensing fees.

- **Technology Transfer:** Explore opportunities for technology transfer and commercialization of intellectual property through partnerships, joint ventures, collaborations, or licensing arrangements with research institutions, universities, or industry collaborators.

5. International Protection Strategies:

- **Global IP Protection:** Implement international IP protection strategies to secure intellectual property rights in key markets and jurisdictions where you conduct business, filing for patents, trademarks, or copyrights in foreign countries or regions to prevent infringement and unauthorized use of your IP assets.

- **International Treaties and Agreements:** Leverage international treaties and agreements, such as the Paris Convention for the Protection of Industrial Property and the Agreement on Trade-Related Aspects of Intellectual Property Rights (TRIPS), to streamline and harmonize IP protection across borders and facilitate cross-border enforcement of intellectual property rights.

Protecting intellectual property rights is vital for safeguarding business value and innovation in today's knowledge-based economy. By identifying assets, securing legal protection, monitoring and enforcing rights, and exploring licensing opportunities, businesses preserve their competitive advantage. Embrace IP protection as strategic, investing in management, enforcement, and commercialization to position for long-term success in the global marketplace.

~~~~~~
~~~~~~

18.1 Building Relationships with Industry Peers and Mentors

Networking and collaboration are essential components of entrepreneurial success, providing opportunities for learning, mentorship, and growth. In this chapter, we explore the importance of building relationships with industry peers and mentors to expand your network, gain valuable insights, and foster professional development.

1. Engaging with Industry Peers:

- **Attend Networking Events:** Participate in industry conferences, trade shows, seminars, and networking events to connect with like-minded professionals, entrepreneurs, and industry leaders who share similar interests, challenges, and aspirations.

- **Join Professional Associations:** Become a member of relevant professional associations, industry groups, or business chambers that cater to your specific sector or niche, leveraging networking platforms, forums, and online communities to engage with peers and exchange knowledge and experiences.

2. Seeking Mentorship and Guidance:

- **Identify Potential Mentors:** Identify experienced professionals, seasoned entrepreneurs, or industry veterans who possess the knowledge, skills, and insights you seek to develop, reaching out to them for mentorship, guidance, and advice on navigating challenges and seizing opportunities.

- **Formal Mentorship Programs:** Participate in formal mentorship programs offered by business incubators, accelerators, academic institutions, or industry associations, pairing aspiring entrepreneurs with seasoned mentors who can provide mentorship, coaching, and support in various aspects of business development.

3. Nurturing Relationships:
- **Build Trust and Rapport:** Invest time and effort in building genuine, authentic relationships with industry peers and mentors based on mutual respect, trust, and shared interests, demonstrating sincerity, integrity, and a willingness to learn and collaborate.

- **Stay Connected and Engaged:** Maintain regular communication and interaction with your network of peers and mentors, staying connected through meetings, calls, emails, or social media platforms, sharing updates, seeking feedback, and offering support as needed.

4. Leveraging Collective Wisdom:
- **Tap into Diverse Perspectives:** Benefit from the diverse perspectives, experiences, and expertise of your network of industry peers and mentors, seeking insights, alternative viewpoints, and innovative solutions to business challenges or opportunities you encounter.

- **Collaborative Learning:** Foster a culture of collaborative learning and knowledge sharing within your network, leveraging peer-to-peer learning, mentorship circles, mastermind groups, or collaborative projects to collectively address common challenges, explore new ideas, and facilitate professional growth.

5. Paying It Forward:

- **Be a Mentor:** Pay forward the knowledge, support, and guidance you receive from your mentors by mentoring aspiring entrepreneurs, emerging professionals, or junior colleagues, sharing your experiences, lessons learned, and best practices to empower others on their entrepreneurial journey.

- **Give Back to the Community:** Contribute to the growth and development of your industry ecosystem or entrepreneurial community by volunteering, organizing events, or participating in initiatives that foster networking, collaboration, and knowledge exchange among peers.

Building relationships with industry peers and mentors is a cornerstone of entrepreneurial success, providing valuable opportunities for learning, growth, and collaboration. By actively engaging with industry peers, seeking mentorship and guidance, nurturing authentic relationships, leveraging collective wisdom, and paying it forward to others, entrepreneurs can expand their networks, gain valuable insights, and accelerate their professional development. Embrace networking and collaboration as essential strategies for building a supportive ecosystem, fostering innovation, and achieving long-term success in your entrepreneurial journey.

~~~~~~
~~~~~~

18.2 Joining Business Associations and Networking Events

Participating in business associations and networking events is a vital strategy for expanding your professional network, fostering collaborations, and gaining valuable insights. In this chapter, we delve into the benefits of joining business associations and attending networking events to enhance your entrepreneurial journey.

1. Identifying Relevant Associations:

- **Research Industry Associations:** Identify industry-specific associations, chambers of commerce, or professional organizations relevant to your business sector or niche, exploring their membership criteria, benefits, and activities to determine alignment with your objectives.

- **Local, National, and International Associations:** Consider joining local, national, or international associations based on your geographic scope, market focus, or industry specialization, leveraging their networks and resources to access opportunities and expertise.

2. Benefits of Association Memberships:

- **Networking Opportunities:** Access exclusive networking platforms, events, and forums facilitated by business associations to connect with industry peers, potential collaborators, investors, and mentors, expanding your professional network and fostering meaningful relationships.

* **Industry Insights and Updates:** Stay abreast of industry trends, market developments, regulatory changes, and best practices through association publications, newsletters, seminars, and educational programs, gaining valuable insights to inform strategic decision-making and business planning.

* **Advocacy and Representation:** Benefit from advocacy efforts, lobbying initiatives, and industry representation conducted by business associations on behalf of their members, influencing policy decisions, shaping regulatory frameworks, and addressing common industry challenges.

3. Leveraging Networking Events:
* **Attend Industry Conferences:** Participate in industry conferences, trade shows, exhibitions, and summits organized by business associations, leveraging these events as opportunities to showcase your business, build brand visibility, and engage with potential partners, customers, and investors.

* **Networking Mixers and Meetups:** Attend networking mixers, meetups, and social gatherings organized by business associations or industry groups, facilitating casual interactions, relationship building, and knowledge exchange in a relaxed and informal setting.

4. Active Participation and Engagement:
* **Join Committees and Task Forces:** Volunteer to serve on committees, task forces, or advisory boards within business associations, contributing your expertise, insights, and leadership skills to drive

initiatives, shape agendas, and address industry issues of mutual interest.

- **Host Workshops and Seminars:** Offer to host workshops, seminars, or educational sessions on topics relevant to your expertise or industry specialization, positioning yourself as a thought leader and subject matter expert within the association community.

5. Building Lasting Relationships:
- **Follow-Up and Follow Through:** Cultivate lasting relationships with fellow association members by following up after networking events, sending personalized follow-up emails, scheduling one-on-one meetings, or connecting on professional networking platforms.

- **Offer Value and Support:** Be proactive in offering value, support, and assistance to fellow association members, sharing resources, making introductions, and providing referrals whenever possible to nurture reciprocal relationships and goodwill within the community.

Business associations and networking events are key for expanding your network, accessing insights, and fostering collaborations. Active participation and relationship-building unlock opportunities, support growth, and accelerate success in the marketplace. Embrace memberships and events as essential for your entrepreneurial journey, investing in meaningful connections and contributing to industry advancement.

~~~~~~
~~~~~~

18.3 Collaborating with Other Businesses for Mutual Benefit

Collaboration with other businesses can be a powerful strategy for accelerating growth, expanding market reach, and fostering innovation. In this chapter, we explore the benefits of collaborating with other businesses for mutual benefit and how to establish successful partnerships.

1. Identifying Collaborative Opportunities:

- **Assess Complementary Capabilities:** Identify businesses with complementary capabilities, resources, or expertise that can enhance your offerings or address gaps in your value proposition, exploring potential synergies and alignment of strategic objectives.

- **Explore Shared Goals and Objectives:** Seek out businesses that share similar goals, values, or target markets, aligning with partners whose interests and aspirations align with yours to facilitate a mutually beneficial collaboration.

2. Types of Collaborative Arrangements:

- **Strategic Alliances:** Form strategic alliances with businesses to jointly pursue opportunities, leverage each other's strengths, and achieve shared objectives, such as co-marketing campaigns, cross-promotional activities, or joint product development initiatives.

- **Partnerships and Joint Ventures:** Establish partnerships or joint ventures with businesses to collaborate on specific projects, ventures, or initiatives, pooling resources, expertise, and risks to achieve common goals and create shared value.

- **Supplier and Vendor Relationships:** Build collaborative relationships with suppliers, vendors, or service providers to optimize supply chain efficiency, streamline operations, and drive mutual business success through strategic partnerships and supplier development programs.

3. Benefits of Business Collaboration:

- **Expanded Market Reach:** Tap into new markets, customer segments, or distribution channels by collaborating with businesses that have established networks, customer bases, or market presence, accelerating market penetration and increasing brand visibility.

- **Enhanced Innovation and Creativity:** Foster innovation, creativity, and problem-solving by bringing together diverse perspectives, skills, and experiences from different businesses, sparking new ideas, insights, and approaches to business challenges or opportunities.

- **Cost Savings and Resource Sharing:** Realize cost savings, economies of scale, and operational efficiencies through resource sharing, shared infrastructure, or joint procurement initiatives, maximizing utilization of resources and minimizing overhead costs.

4. Establishing Successful Collaborations:

- **Clear Objectives and Expectations:** Define clear objectives, roles, responsibilities, and expectations for the collaboration, establishing a shared vision and agreement on key deliverables, timelines, and success metrics to guide the partnership.

- **Open Communication and Trust:** Foster open communication, transparency, and trust between collaborating parties, maintaining regular dialogue, feedback loops, and conflict resolution mechanisms to address issues and ensure alignment throughout the collaboration.

- **Flexibility and Adaptability:** Remain flexible and adaptable in navigating changes, challenges, or opportunities that may arise during the collaboration, demonstrating agility, resilience, and a willingness to adjust strategies or course correct as needed to achieve shared goals.

5. Evaluating Collaboration Success:

- **Performance Metrics and KPIs:** Establish performance metrics, key performance indicators (KPIs), or benchmarks to measure the success and impact of the collaboration, tracking outcomes, ROI, and other relevant indicators to assess effectiveness and inform future decision-making.

- **Continuous Improvement:** Continuously evaluate and review the collaboration process, outcomes, and lessons learned, soliciting feedback from all stakeholders, and identifying areas for improvement or optimization to enhance the value and sustainability of future collaborations.

Collaborating with other businesses for mutual benefit is a strategic imperative for entrepreneurs seeking to accelerate growth, drive innovation, and create shared value in the marketplace. By identifying collaborative opportunities, establishing successful partnerships, and leveraging the collective strengths and resources of collaborating parties, businesses can unlock new growth opportunities, expand market reach, and achieve greater impact and success together. Embrace collaboration as a cornerstone of your business strategy, actively seeking out opportunities to collaborate with like-minded partners and realizing the transformative power of collective action in achieving shared goals and driving positive change in the business ecosystem.

~~~~~~
~~~~~~

19.1 Setting Key Performance Indicators (KPIs) for Business Success

Setting Key Performance Indicators (KPIs) is essential for measuring and evaluating the performance of your business against strategic objectives and targets. In this chapter, we explore the importance of setting KPIs and provide guidance on identifying, defining, and tracking KPIs for business success.

1. Understanding Key Performance Indicators (KPIs):

- **Definition and Purpose:** Define KPIs as quantifiable metrics used to measure performance and progress towards achieving specific business goals, objectives, or outcomes, providing actionable insights to inform decision-making and drive continuous improvement.

- **Strategic Alignment:** Ensure alignment between KPIs and strategic objectives, identifying KPIs that directly reflect the critical success factors, priorities, and desired outcomes of your business strategy.

2. Identifying Relevant KPIs:

- **Strategic Focus Areas:** Identify key focus areas or functional areas of your business where KPIs are needed to monitor performance and track progress, such as sales, marketing, operations, finance, customer service, or employee productivity.

- **SMART Criteria:** Apply the SMART criteria (Specific, Measurable, Achievable, Relevant, Time-bound) to define KPIs that are specific, quantifiable, realistic, relevant to business objectives, and time-bound for tracking progress and performance.

3. Types of Business KPIs:
- **Financial KPIs:** Measure financial performance and profitability metrics, such as revenue growth, gross margin, net profit margin, return on investment (ROI), cash flow, and working capital ratio.

- **Operational KPIs:** Track operational efficiency, productivity, and performance metrics, including production output, inventory turnover, lead time, cycle time, resource utilization, and process efficiency.

- **Customer KPIs:** Assess customer satisfaction, loyalty, and engagement metrics, such as Net Promoter Score (NPS), customer retention rate, customer lifetime value (CLV), and customer acquisition cost (CAC).

- **Marketing KPIs:** Evaluate marketing effectiveness and ROI metrics, such as website traffic, conversion rate, customer acquisition rate, marketing ROI, and brand awareness.

- **Employee KPIs:** Monitor employee performance, engagement, and satisfaction indicators, including employee turnover rate, absenteeism, employee satisfaction surveys, and performance reviews.

4. Defining KPI Targets and Benchmarks:
- **Baseline Measurement:** Establish baseline measurements and historical data for each KPI to set realistic targets, benchmarks, or thresholds for performance improvement and goal attainment.

- **Stretch Goals:** Set stretch goals or aspirational targets to challenge your business to achieve higher levels of performance and drive continuous improvement over time.

5. Tracking and Monitoring KPIs:
- **Data Collection and Analysis:** Implement systems, processes, or tools for collecting, aggregating, and analyzing KPI data in real-time or at regular intervals, enabling timely insights and informed decision-making.

- **Dashboard Reporting:** Utilize KPI dashboards or scorecards to visually display performance metrics, trends, and progress towards targets, facilitating easy interpretation and communication of results to stakeholders.

6. Reviewing and Adjusting KPIs:
- **Regular Performance Reviews:** Conduct regular reviews and evaluations of KPI performance against targets, analyzing variances, identifying root causes of deviations, and taking corrective actions or adjustments as necessary.

- **Continuous Improvement:** Foster a culture of continuous improvement and learning, leveraging KPI insights to drive strategic initiatives, process optimization, and organizational development efforts aimed at achieving business success.

Setting Key Performance Indicators (KPIs) is a critical step in evaluating business performance, driving accountability, and achieving strategic objectives. By identifying relevant KPIs, defining clear targets and benchmarks, tracking and monitoring performance metrics, and reviewing and adjusting KPIs based on insights and feedback, businesses can effectively measure progress, drive performance improvement, and ultimately achieve long-term success and sustainability. Embrace KPIs as a powerful tool for driving performance excellence, guiding decision-making, and maximizing business impact in pursuit of your entrepreneurial goals and aspirations.

~~~~~~~~~~~~~~~~~~~~~~~~~~~~~~~~~~
~~~~~~~~~~~~~~~~~~~~~~~~~~~~~~~~~~

19.2 Monitoring and Analyzing Financial and Operational Metrics

Monitoring and analyzing financial and operational metrics is essential for assessing the health, performance, and viability of your business. In this chapter, we delve into the importance of monitoring and analyzing these metrics and provide guidance on how to effectively leverage them for business evaluation and improvement.

1. Financial Metrics:

- **Revenue Growth:** Track the rate at which your business's revenue is increasing over time, assessing the effectiveness of sales and marketing efforts in driving business growth.

- **Profitability Ratios:** Analyze profitability ratios such as gross profit margin, net profit margin, and return on investment (ROI) to evaluate the efficiency and profitability of your business operations.

- **Cash Flow Management:** Monitor cash flow metrics including cash flow from operations, investing, and financing activities to ensure adequate liquidity and financial stability.

- **Financial Health Indicators:** Assess financial health indicators such as working capital ratio, debt-to-equity ratio, and current ratio to gauge your business's financial strength and solvency.

2. Operational Metrics:

- **Production Efficiency:** Measure production efficiency metrics such as production output, cycle time, and defect rate to assess the effectiveness of your manufacturing or production processes.
- **Inventory Management:** Monitor inventory turnover ratio, days sales of inventory (DSI), and inventory carrying costs to optimize inventory levels and minimize holding costs.

- **Customer Service Performance:** Track customer service metrics including response time, resolution time, and customer satisfaction scores to ensure high-quality customer service and satisfaction.

- **Employee Productivity:** Analyze employee productivity metrics such as revenue per employee, labor cost per unit, and employee turnover rate to optimize workforce efficiency and performance.

3. Monitoring Tools and Systems:

- **Accounting Software:** Utilize accounting software to streamline financial recordkeeping, automate transaction processing, and generate financial reports for analysis and decision-making.

- **Enterprise Resource Planning (ERP) Systems:** Implement ERP systems to integrate and manage core business processes including finance, inventory management, production, and customer relationship management (CRM).

- **Business Intelligence (BI) Tools:** Leverage BI tools and dashboards to visualize and analyze financial and operational data, uncover insights, and make data-driven decisions to drive business performance.

4. Analytical Techniques:

- **Trend Analysis:** Conduct trend analysis to identify patterns, trends, and anomalies in financial and operational data over time, gaining insights into performance trends and forecasting future outcomes.

- **Variance Analysis:** Perform variance analysis to compare actual performance against budgeted or target values, identifying variances and investigating root causes to take corrective actions.

- **Benchmarking:** Benchmark your business's financial and operational metrics against industry peers or best practices to assess performance relative to competitors and identify areas for improvement.

5. Actionable Insights and Decision-Making:

- **Data-Driven Decision-Making:** Use insights from financial and operational metrics to inform strategic decision-making, prioritize initiatives, and allocate resources effectively to drive business growth and profitability.

- **Continuous Improvement:** Embrace a culture of continuous improvement, leveraging insights from monitoring and analysis to identify opportunities for optimization, innovation, and operational excellence to enhance business performance over time.

Monitoring and analyzing financial and operational metrics are critical practices for evaluating business performance, identifying areas for improvement, and driving strategic decision-making. By effectively monitoring key financial and operational metrics, leveraging analytical tools and techniques, and translating insights into actionable strategies, entrepreneurs can optimize business performance, mitigate risks, and achieve sustainable growth and success in today's competitive landscape. Embrace financial and operational metrics as invaluable tools for driving business excellence and maximizing the long-term success and viability of your business.

~~~~~~~~~~~~~~~~~~~~~~~~
~~~~~~~~~~~~~~~~~~~~~~~~

19.3 Conducting Regular Business Reviews and Assessments

Regular business reviews and assessments are essential for evaluating performance, identifying areas for improvement, and driving strategic decision-making. In this chapter, we explore the importance of conducting these reviews and provide guidance on how to effectively assess and optimize your business operations.

1. Establishing Review Cycles:

- **Frequency:** Determine the frequency of business reviews based on the nature of your business, industry dynamics, and strategic objectives. Reviews may occur monthly, quarterly, or annually.

- **Consistency:** Maintain consistency in review cycles to ensure timely assessment of performance and alignment with strategic goals.

2. Key Areas of Assessment:

- **Financial Performance:** Evaluate financial metrics such as revenue, profit margins, cash flow, and return on investment (ROI) to assess the overall financial health and profitability of the business.

- **Operational Efficiency:** Assess operational metrics including production output, inventory management, and resource utilization to identify opportunities for streamlining processes and improving efficiency.

- **Customer Satisfaction:** Measure customer satisfaction scores, feedback, and retention rates to gauge the effectiveness of customer service efforts and identify areas for enhancing the customer experience.

- **Employee Engagement:** Review employee satisfaction surveys, turnover rates, and performance metrics to evaluate workforce engagement and identify opportunities for talent development and retention.

3. Performance Against KPIs:

- **Key Performance Indicators (KPIs):** Evaluate performance against predefined KPIs to track progress towards strategic objectives and identify areas of strength and improvement.

- **Variance Analysis:** Conduct variance analysis to compare actual performance against targets or benchmarks, identifying deviations and exploring root causes for corrective action.

4. SWOT Analysis:

- **Strengths:** Identify internal strengths and competitive advantages that contribute to the business's success and differentiation in the market.

- **Weaknesses:** Recognize areas of weakness or vulnerability that may hinder business performance or pose risks to achieving strategic objectives.

- **Opportunities:** Identify external opportunities for growth, expansion, or innovation that the business can leverage to capitalize on market trends or emerging demand.

- **Threats:** Assess external threats and risks that may impact the business, such as competitive pressures, market volatility, or regulatory changes.

5. Action Planning:
- **Prioritization:** Prioritize areas for improvement based on the findings of the business review and assessment process, focusing on initiatives that will have the greatest impact on business performance and strategic goals.

- **Actionable Goals:** Establish clear, actionable goals and objectives for addressing identified weaknesses, capitalizing on opportunities, and mitigating threats.

- **Implementation:** Develop action plans outlining specific tasks, timelines, and responsibilities for executing improvement initiatives and monitoring progress.

6. Continuous Improvement:
- **Feedback Loop:** Establish a feedback loop for continuous improvement, soliciting input from stakeholders, monitoring results, and adjusting strategies and tactics as needed.

- **Learning Culture:** Foster a culture of learning and adaptability within the organization, encouraging innovation, experimentation, and ongoing skill development to stay ahead in a dynamic business environment.

Conducting regular business reviews and assessments is essential for evaluating performance, identifying opportunities, and driving continuous improvement. By systematically reviewing financial and operational metrics, assessing performance against KPIs, conducting SWOT analyses, and developing action plans for improvement, businesses can optimize their operations, enhance competitiveness, and achieve sustainable growth and success. Embrace the business review process as a strategic imperative for driving performance excellence and realizing your business's full potential.

~~~~~~~~~~~~~~~~~~~~
~~~~~~~~~~~~~~~~~~~~

Chapter 20: Celebrating Success & Continued Learning

20.1 Recognizing Milestones and Achievements

Celebrating milestones and achievements is vital for fostering a positive company culture, boosting morale, and reinforcing the commitment to success. In this chapter, we explore the importance of recognizing milestones and achievements and provide guidance on how to effectively celebrate success within your business.

1. Importance of Recognition:
- **Motivation:** Recognizing milestones and achievements motivates employees, reinforcing their efforts and encouraging continued dedication to excellence.

- **Engagement:** Celebrating success fosters a sense of belonging and engagement among team members, strengthening bonds and promoting collaboration.

- **Retention:** Acknowledging accomplishments helps retain top talent by making employees feel valued and appreciated for their contributions.

2. Types of Milestones and Achievements:
- **Business Milestones:** Celebrate significant business achievements such as reaching revenue targets, launching new products or services, or expanding into new markets.

- **Employee Accomplishments:** Recognize individual and team accomplishments, including meeting project deadlines, surpassing sales quotas, or earning certifications or awards.

- **Customer Success:** Celebrate customer milestones, such as long-term partnerships, positive feedback, or testimonials, highlighting the impact of your products or services on their businesses.

3. Effective Recognition Strategies:
- **Personalized Recognition:** Tailor recognition efforts to individual preferences and motivations, considering factors such as public praise, monetary rewards, or personalized thank-you notes.

- **Timely Recognition:** Provide timely recognition for achievements, acknowledging successes promptly to reinforce positive behaviors and outcomes.

- **Peer Recognition:** Encourage peer-to-peer recognition, empowering employees to recognize and celebrate each other's contributions, fostering a culture of appreciation and support.

4. Celebration Activities:
- **Team Events:** Organize team events or outings to celebrate milestones and achievements, such as team lunches, dinners, or off-site activities, promoting camaraderie and team spirit.

- **Recognition Ceremonies:** Host formal recognition ceremonies or awards ceremonies to honor outstanding achievements, publicly acknowledging recipients and their contributions.

- **Virtual Celebrations:** In remote or virtual work environments, leverage video conferencing tools to host virtual celebrations, including virtual happy hours, team games, or recognition shout-outs.

5. Continued Learning and Growth:
- **Reflection:** Use milestone celebrations as an opportunity for reflection and learning, discussing lessons learned, challenges overcome, and opportunities for improvement.
- **Goal Setting:** Set new goals and objectives for the future, building on past achievements and charting a course for continued growth and success.

- **Professional Development:** Invest in employee development and training initiatives, supporting ongoing learning and skill enhancement to prepare for future challenges and opportunities.

6. Cultivating a Culture of Success:
- **Consistency:** Make recognition and celebration a consistent practice within your organization, embedding it into the company culture and values.

- **Leadership Example:** Lead by example, demonstrating appreciation and recognition for achievements at all levels of the organization, from frontline employees to senior leadership.

- **Feedback Loop:** Solicit feedback from employees on recognition efforts, seeking input on what types of recognition are most meaningful and impactful to them, and adjusting strategies accordingly.

Recognizing milestones and achievements is essential for fostering a culture of success, engagement, and continuous improvement within your business. By celebrating successes, acknowledging contributions, and promoting a culture of appreciation and recognition, you can motivate employees, strengthen teamwork, and drive sustained performance and growth. Embrace recognition as a strategic tool for building morale, retaining talent, and propelling your business towards greater success and prosperity.

~~~~~~~~~~~~~~~~~~~~~~~~~~~~
~~~~~~~~~~~~~~~~~~~~~~~~~~~~

20.2 Embracing a Culture of Continuous Improvement and Learning

In this chapter, we delve into the importance of fostering a culture of continuous improvement and learning within your organization. We explore strategies for promoting ongoing growth, innovation, and development to drive long-term success.

1. Understanding Continuous Improvement:
- **Definition:** Continuous improvement involves ongoing efforts to enhance processes, products, and services incrementally over time.

- **Kaizen Philosophy:** Embrace the Kaizen philosophy of continuous improvement, which emphasizes small, incremental changes and a commitment to excellence in all aspects of the business.

2. Benefits of Continuous Improvement:
- **Enhanced Efficiency:** Continuous improvement initiatives streamline processes, eliminate waste, and optimize resource utilization, leading to greater efficiency and productivity.

- **Innovation:** Foster a culture of innovation by encouraging experimentation, creativity, and the pursuit of new ideas and solutions.

- **Adaptability:** Continuously improving allows your organization to adapt to changing market conditions, customer preferences, and industry trends, ensuring relevance and competitiveness.

3. Strategies for Continuous Improvement:

- **Employee Involvement:** Encourage employees at all levels to contribute ideas for improvement, empowering them to take ownership of their work and drive positive change.

- **Process Optimization:** Conduct regular process reviews and assessments to identify inefficiencies, bottlenecks, and areas for improvement, implementing changes to enhance effectiveness and streamline operations.

- **Feedback Mechanisms:** Establish feedback mechanisms such as suggestion boxes, surveys, and performance evaluations to gather input from employees, customers, and other stakeholders, leveraging insights to inform improvement efforts.

- **Benchmarking:** Benchmark your organization against industry peers and best practices, identifying opportunities for improvement and setting targets for performance excellence.

4. Learning and Development Initiatives:

- **Training Programs:** Invest in employee training and development programs to enhance skills, knowledge, and capabilities, enabling employees to perform at their best and contribute to organizational success.

- **Cross-Functional Collaboration:** Encourage collaboration and knowledge sharing across departments and teams, fostering a culture of learning and collaboration.

- **External Resources:** Tap into external resources such as industry events, conferences, and workshops to stay informed about emerging trends, technologies, and best practices, fostering a culture of continuous learning and innovation.

5. Measurement and Evaluation:

- **Key Performance Indicators (KPIs):** Establish KPIs to measure the effectiveness of continuous improvement initiatives, tracking progress and outcomes over time.

- **Feedback Loops:** Implement feedback loops to solicit input from stakeholders and evaluate the impact of improvement efforts, making adjustments as needed to drive further progress.

6. Leadership Support and Commitment:

- **Lead by Example:** Demonstrate a commitment to continuous improvement and learning as a leader, setting the tone for the organization and inspiring others to embrace a culture of growth and excellence.

- **Resource Allocation:** Allocate resources and support for continuous improvement initiatives, providing the necessary tools, training, and incentives to empower employees and drive meaningful change.

Embracing a culture of continuous improvement and learning is essential for driving long-term success and competitiveness in today's dynamic business environment. By fostering a culture of innovation, collaboration, and ongoing growth, organizations can adapt to change, seize opportunities, and achieve excellence in all aspects of their operations. Embrace continuous improvement as a strategic imperative, empowering your organization to thrive and excel in the face of evolving challenges and opportunities.

~~~~~~~~~~~~~~~~~~~~~~~~~~~~~~~~~~~~
~~~~~~~~~~~~~~~~~~~~~~~~~~~~~~~~~~~~

Chapter 20: Celebrating Success and Continued Learning

20.3 Planning for Future Growth and Expansion

In this chapter, we explore the importance of strategic planning for future growth and expansion. We discuss essential considerations, strategies, and steps to prepare your business for sustained success and scalability.

1. Assessing Growth Opportunities:
- **Market Analysis:** Conduct a comprehensive analysis of market trends, customer needs, and competitive dynamics to identify growth opportunities and emerging market segments.

- **SWOT Analysis:** Evaluate your business's strengths, weaknesses, opportunities, and threats to identify areas for growth and potential challenges to address.

2. Setting Growth Objectives:
- **SMART Goals:** Establish Specific, Measurable, Achievable, Relevant, and Time-bound (SMART) goals for future growth, aligning objectives with your organization's vision and strategic priorities.

- **Quantitative Targets:** Define quantitative targets for key performance indicators (KPIs) such as revenue growth, market share expansion, and customer acquisition.

3. Developing a Growth Strategy:
- **Market Penetration:** Explore opportunities to increase market share and customer base within existing markets through targeted marketing

campaigns, product/service enhancements, and competitive pricing strategies.

- **Market Development:** Expand into new geographical regions or target market segments to diversify your customer base and mitigate risks associated with market saturation or economic downturns.

- **Product/Service Innovation:** Invest in research and development to innovate and differentiate your offerings, staying ahead of competitors and meeting evolving customer needs.

4. Assessing Resource Requirements:

- **Financial Planning:** Conduct a thorough financial analysis to assess the capital requirements for future growth initiatives, including investments in infrastructure, technology, marketing, and talent acquisition.

- **Human Resources:** Evaluate your organization's talent needs and capabilities to support growth objectives, identifying areas where additional skills, expertise, or capacity may be required.

5. Mitigating Risks and Challenges:

- **Risk Management:** Identify potential risks and challenges associated with growth and expansion, such as market volatility, regulatory changes, and resource constraints, and develop mitigation strategies to address them.

- **Contingency Planning:** Anticipate potential obstacles or setbacks along the growth journey and develop contingency plans to minimize their impact on business operations and objectives.

6. Monitoring and Adjusting Strategies:

- **Performance Tracking:** Implement systems and processes to track progress towards growth objectives, regularly monitoring key performance indicators (KPIs) and adjusting strategies as needed to stay on course.

- **Adaptability:** Remain flexible and adaptable in response to changing market conditions, customer preferences, and competitive dynamics, pivoting strategies as necessary to capitalize on emerging opportunities and mitigate threats.

Planning for future growth and expansion is essential for sustaining success and competitiveness in today's dynamic business landscape. By assessing growth opportunities, setting clear objectives, developing strategic growth strategies, and mitigating risks, businesses can position themselves for long-term viability and prosperity. Embrace growth planning as a strategic imperative, empowering your organization to seize opportunities, overcome challenges, and achieve sustained growth and excellence.

~~~~~~~~~~~~~~~~~~~~~~~~~~~~
~~~~~~~~~~~~~~~~~~~~~~~~~~~~

Good Luck!

 As we reach the end of this journey through the intricacies of starting a business in India, it's important to reflect on the wealth of knowledge and insights gained along the way. From laying the groundwork with self-assessment and goal setting to navigating the complexities of market research and ideation, each chapter has been a steppingstone towards entrepreneurial success.

Starting a business is not merely about having a great idea or access to resources—it's about having the right mindset, skills, and strategies to turn that idea into a reality. It's about embracing challenges, seizing opportunities, and continuously learning and adapting in a dynamic and ever-changing landscape.

However, it's important to note that while diligence and determination are essential, success in entrepreneurship also requires an element of serendipity. Luck, or what some may call "God's grace," can play a significant role in the journey towards success.

As you embark on your entrepreneurial journey, remember that success is not guaranteed, and setbacks are inevitable. But with perseverance, resilience, and a relentless pursuit of excellence, you have the power to overcome obstacles and achieve greatness.

May this book serve as a guiding light on your path to entrepreneurial success, empowering you to realize your dreams, make a meaningful impact, and leave a lasting legacy in the world of business.

~~~~~~~~~~~~~~~~~~~~~~
~~~~~~~~~~~~~~~~~~~~~~

Disclaimer: The information provided in this book is for educational and informational purposes only. While every effort has been made to ensure accuracy, the author and publisher make no representations or warranties with respect to the accuracy or completeness of the contents. The use of any information provided in this book is at the reader's own risk, and the author and publisher shall not be held liable for any damages or losses arising from the use of this information. Readers are advised to seek professional advice and conduct their own due diligence before making any business decisions.

Here's to your success, and may your entrepreneurial journey be filled with growth, fulfillment, and boundless opportunities. Thanks!

www.ingramcontent.com/pod-product-compliance
Lightning Source LLC
Chambersburg PA
CBHW020841150726
48196CB00002B/171